HIYAAA GUYS !!

THANK YOU SO MUCH
FOR BUYING THIS
I HOPE YOU WILL
ENJOY THIS !! ♡♡

LOVE YA !
@RETNOLARAS

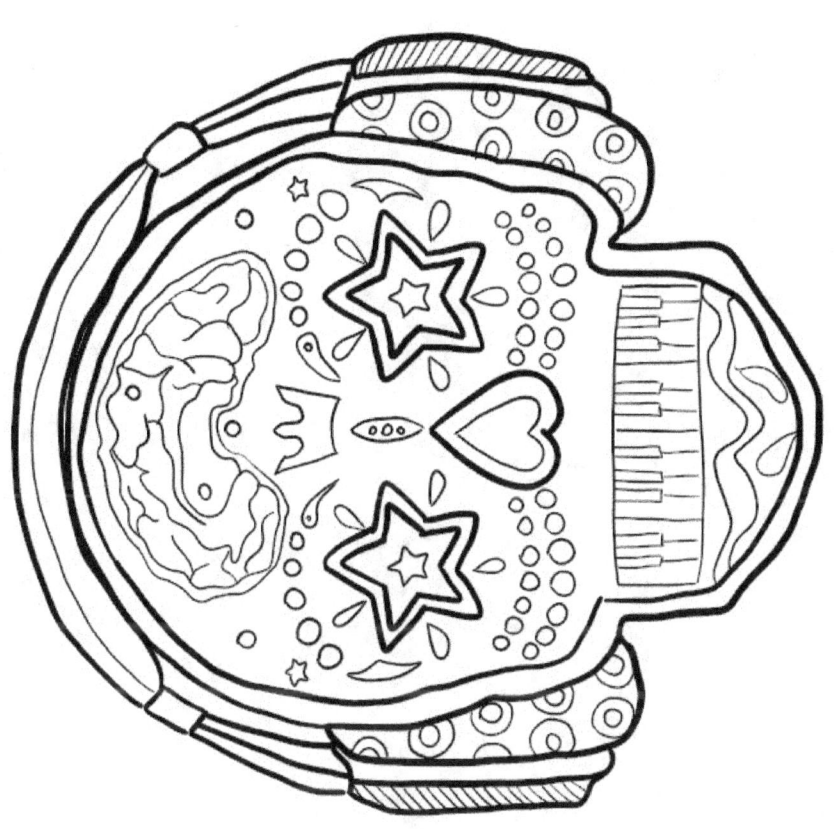

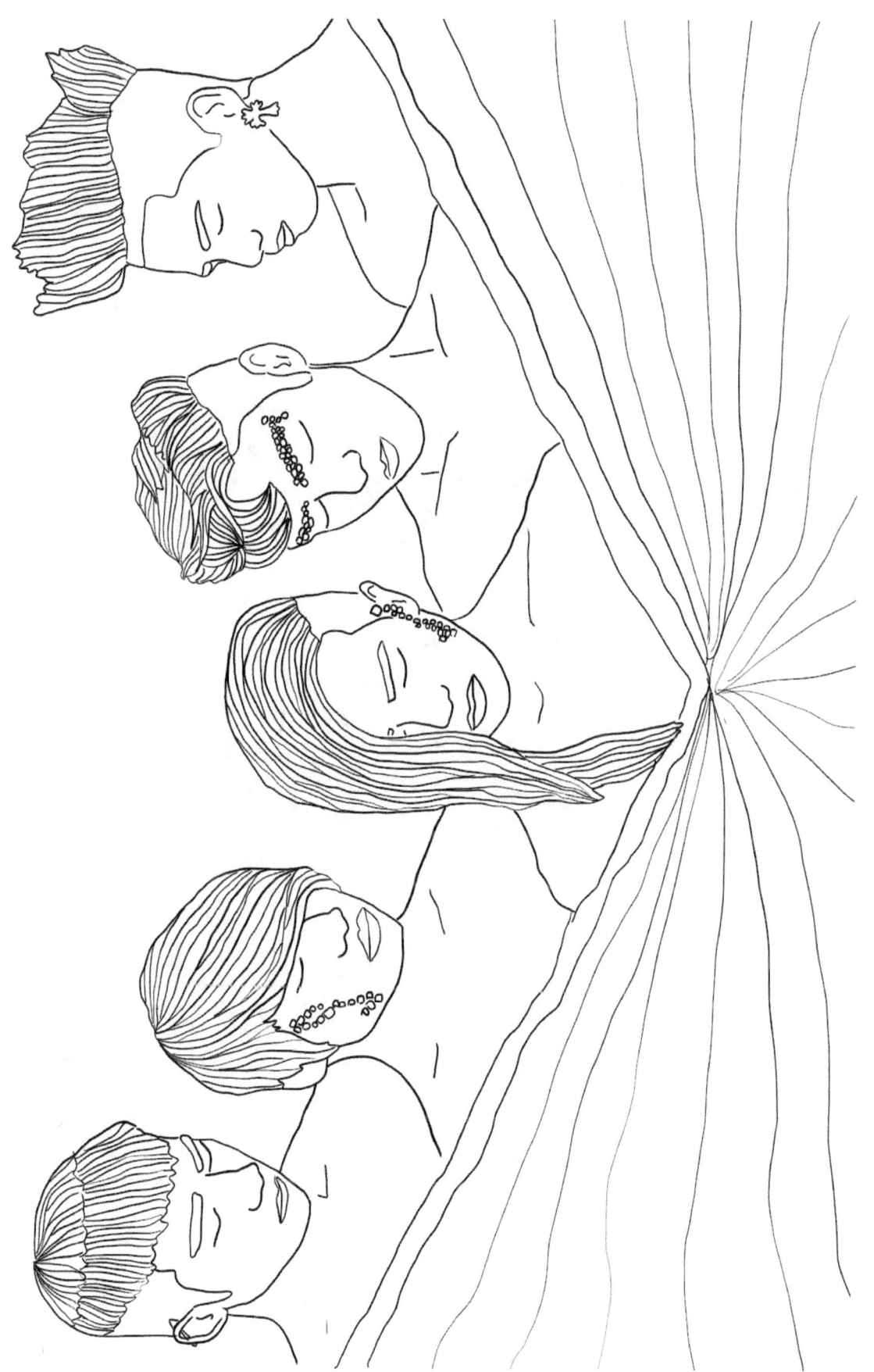

GET READY FOR THE

QUIZ

IF YOU REALLY VIP
YOU KNOW THE
ANSWERS FORTHIS

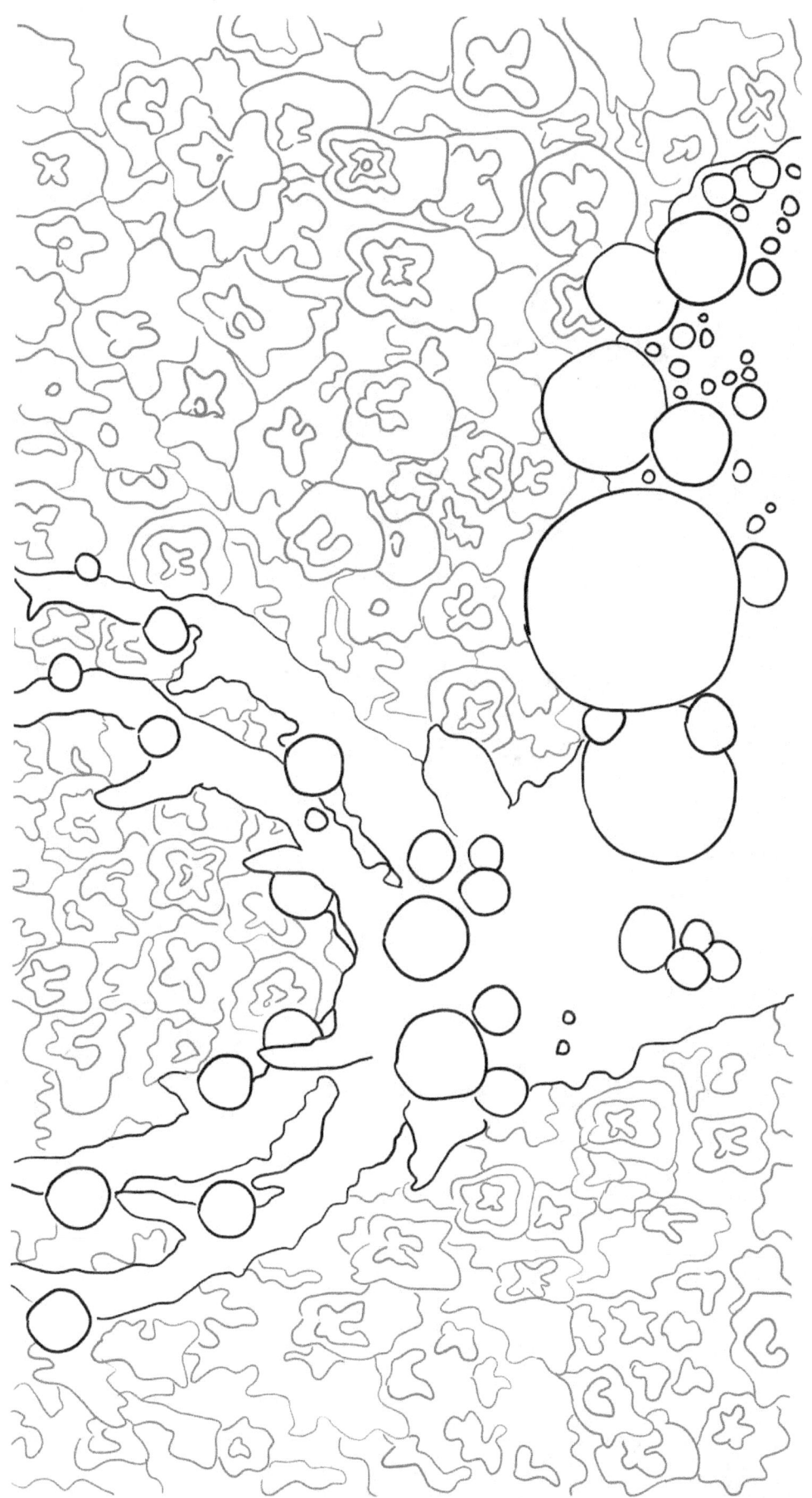

"DON'T BELIEVE IN SUCCESS. RATHER THAN THAT, BELIEVE IN THE AMOUNT OF YOUR ___ AND ___ ." — SEUNGRI

A. FISH AND CHIPS

B. EFFORT AND PASSION

C. TOM AND JERRY

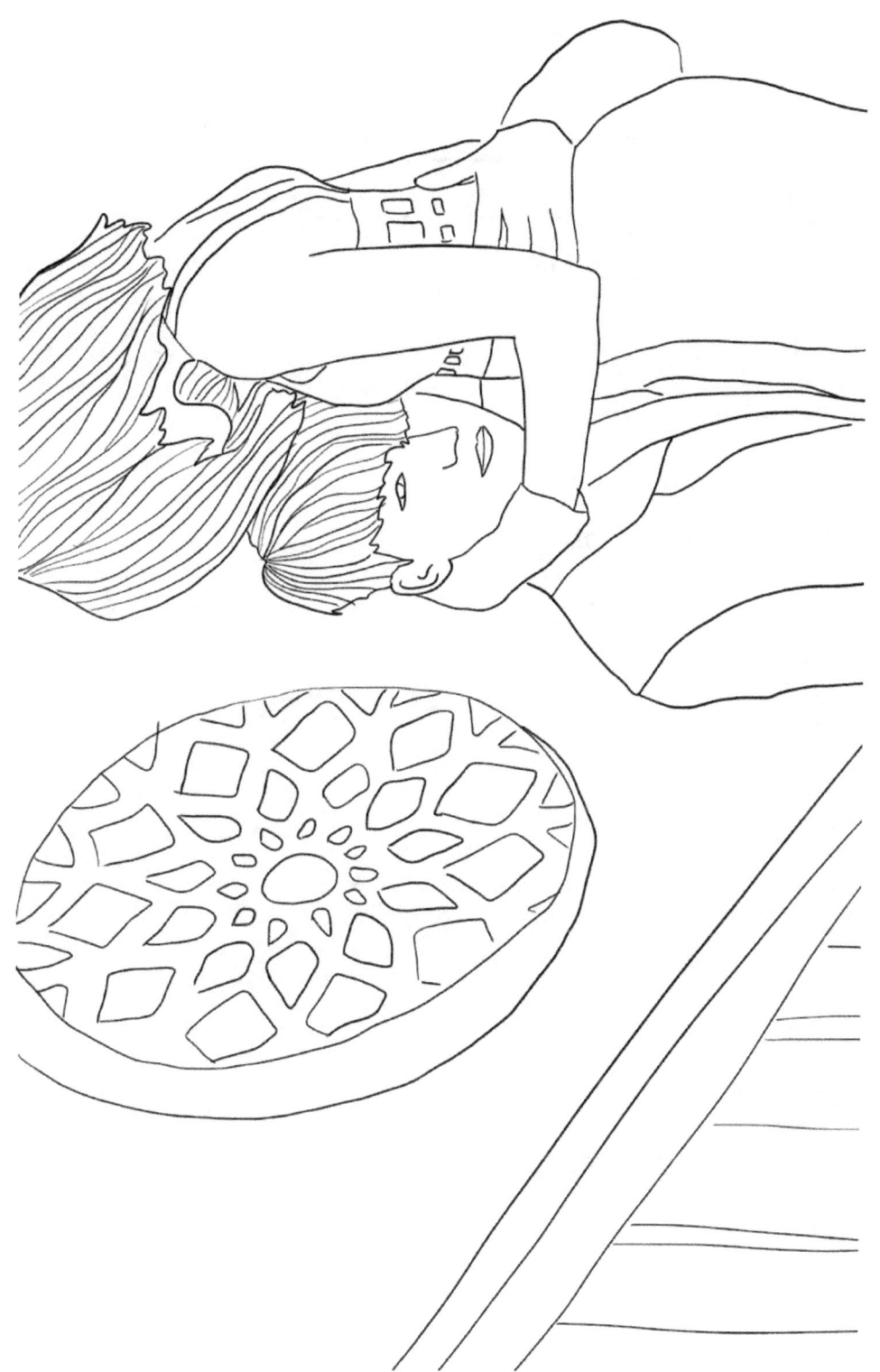

"AN OPEN ____ IS THE
SECRET OF MAKING FRIENDS"
— SEUNGRI

A. FLY
B. SKY
C. MIND

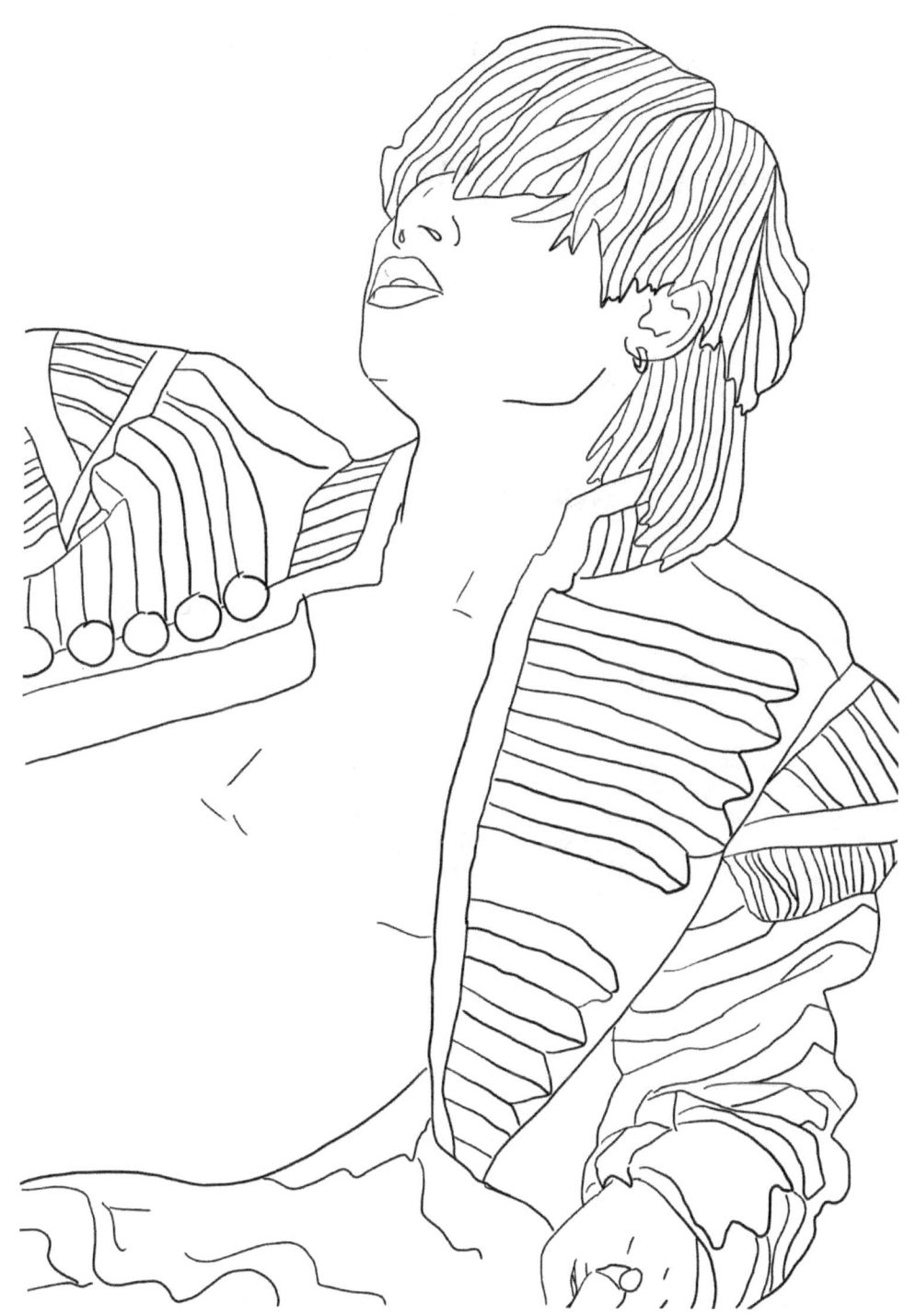

"MY GOAL IS TO BECOME A SINGER
WHO DELIVERS _____ TO
PEOPLE." — DAESUNG

A. HAPPINESS
B. SAPPINESS
C. LONELINESS

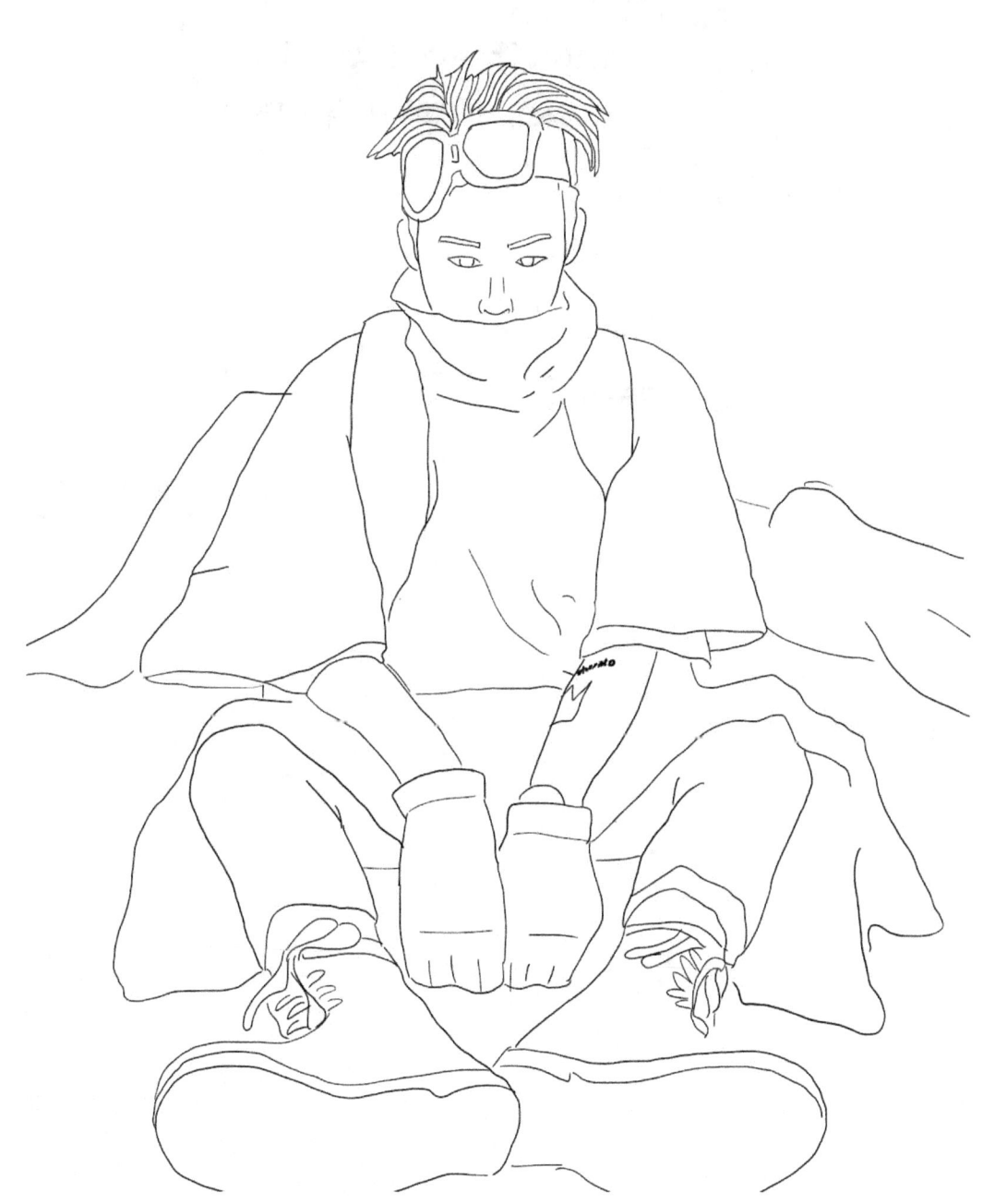

"I HAVE A GOOD PRONUNCIATION
NO MATTER WHAT LANGUAGE I SPEAK.
MAYBE IT'S BECAUSE MY SPECIALITIES
ARE _____ AND IMITATING OTHERS"
— GDRAGON

    A. RAPPING
    B. WRAPPING
    C. FAPING

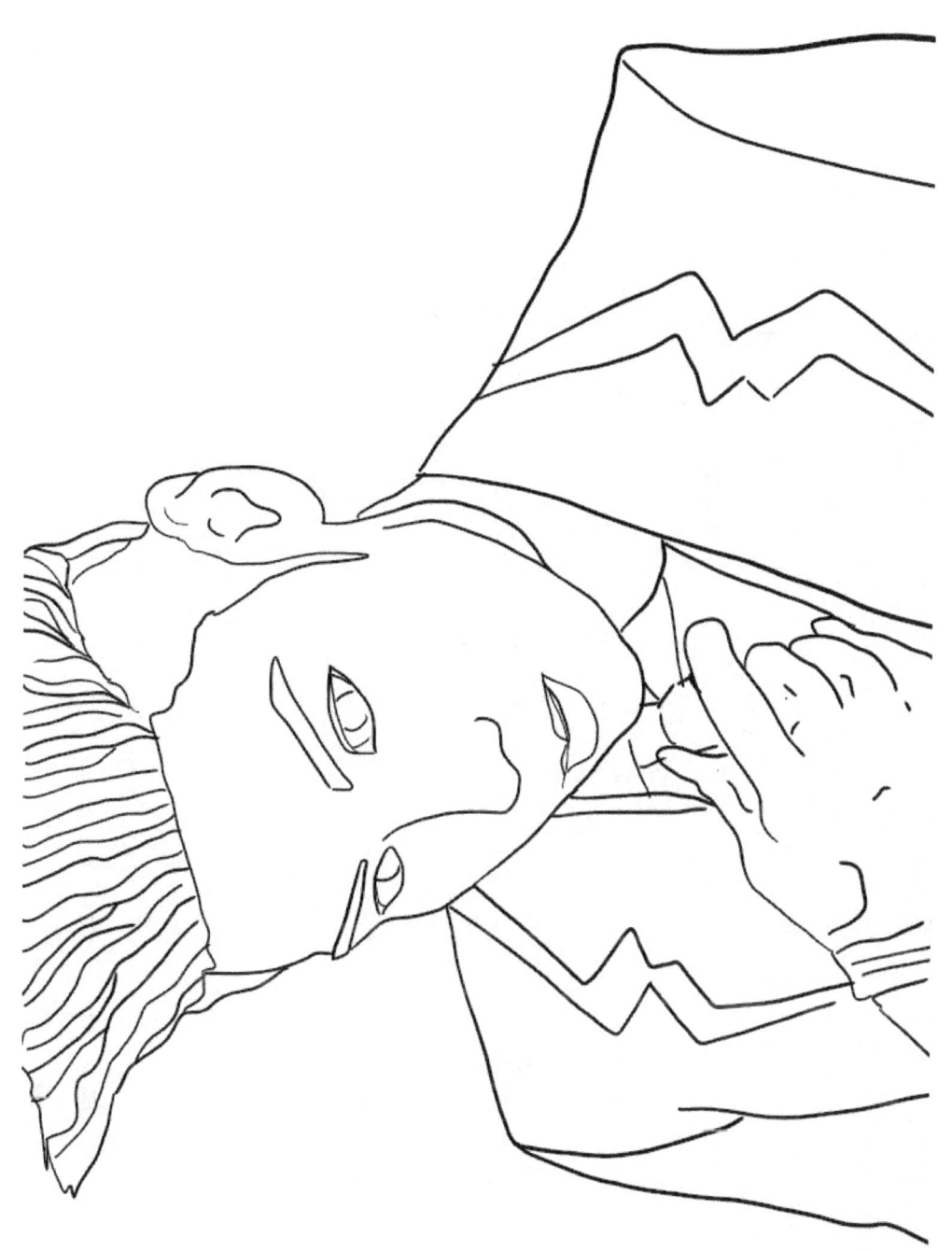

"THE JAPANESE STAR I WANT
TO WORK WITH? _____"

– T.O.P

A. TAKUYA KIMURA
B. YOSHINOYA
C. PIKACHU

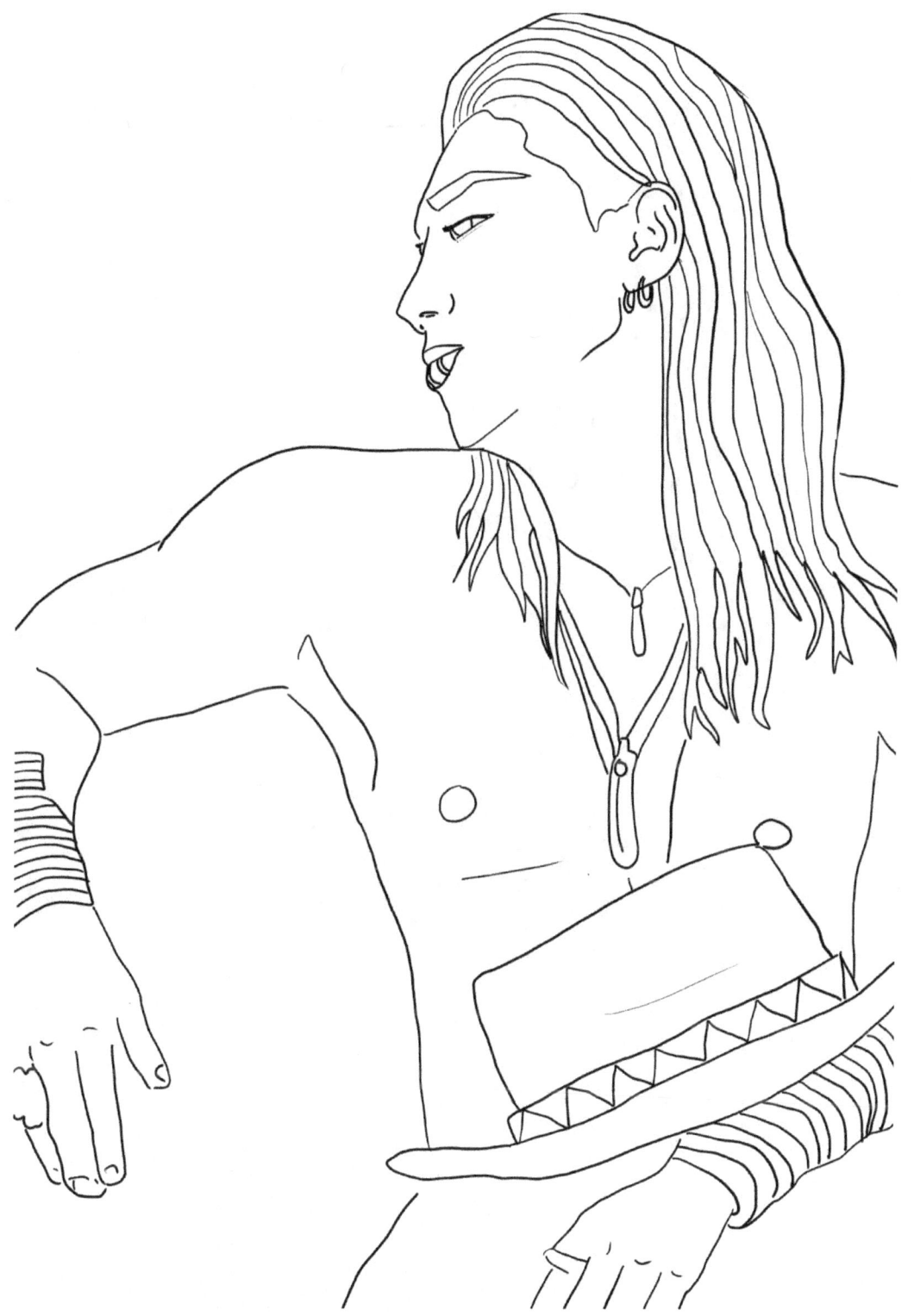

"DOPE VIDEO, _____!"

    – TAEYANG

A. CONGRATS
B. RUGRATS
C. NOUGATS

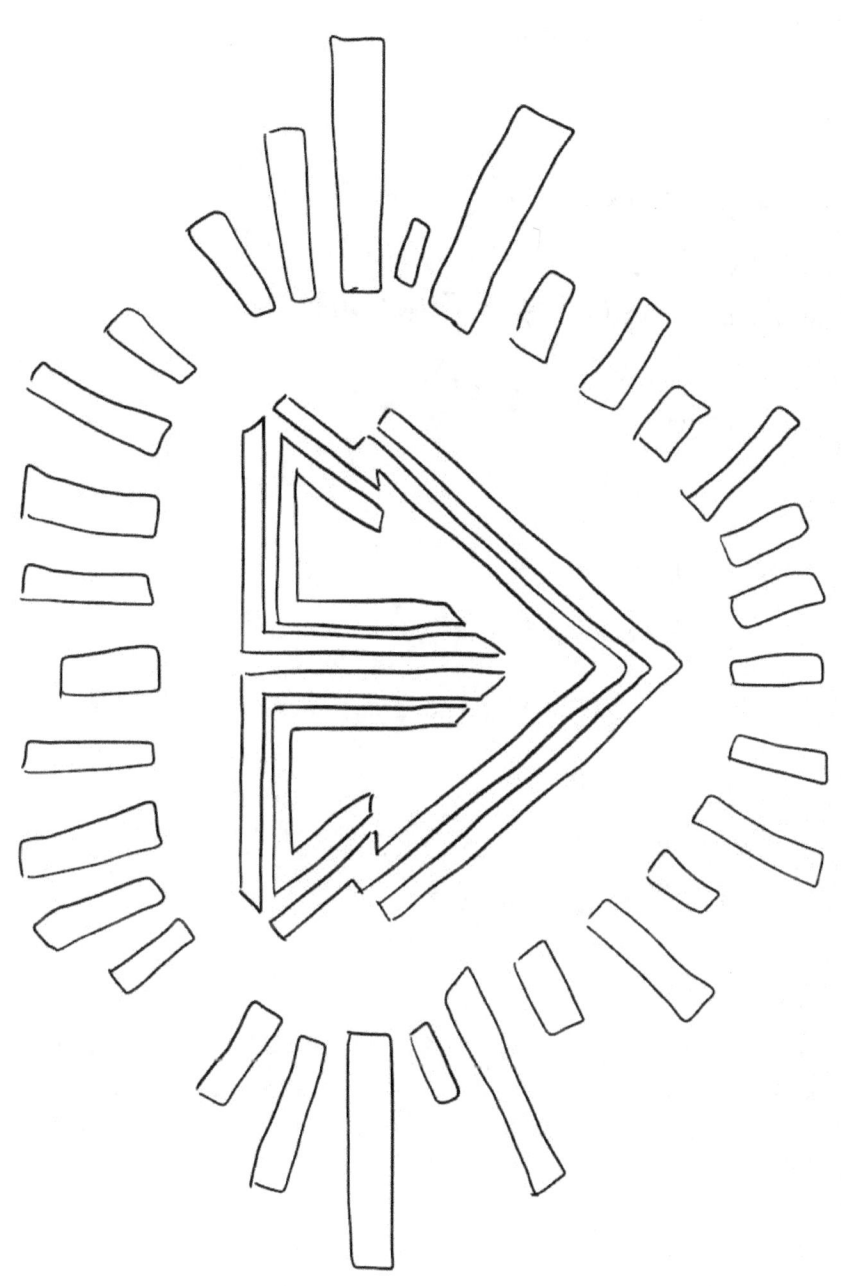

"PEOPLE EXPRESS THEIR FEELINGS
THROUGH CRYING OR ANGER. WE,
BIGBANG, EXPRESS IT THROUGH

_____." — DAESUNG

A. TEARS
B. THE NIGHT
C. MUSIC

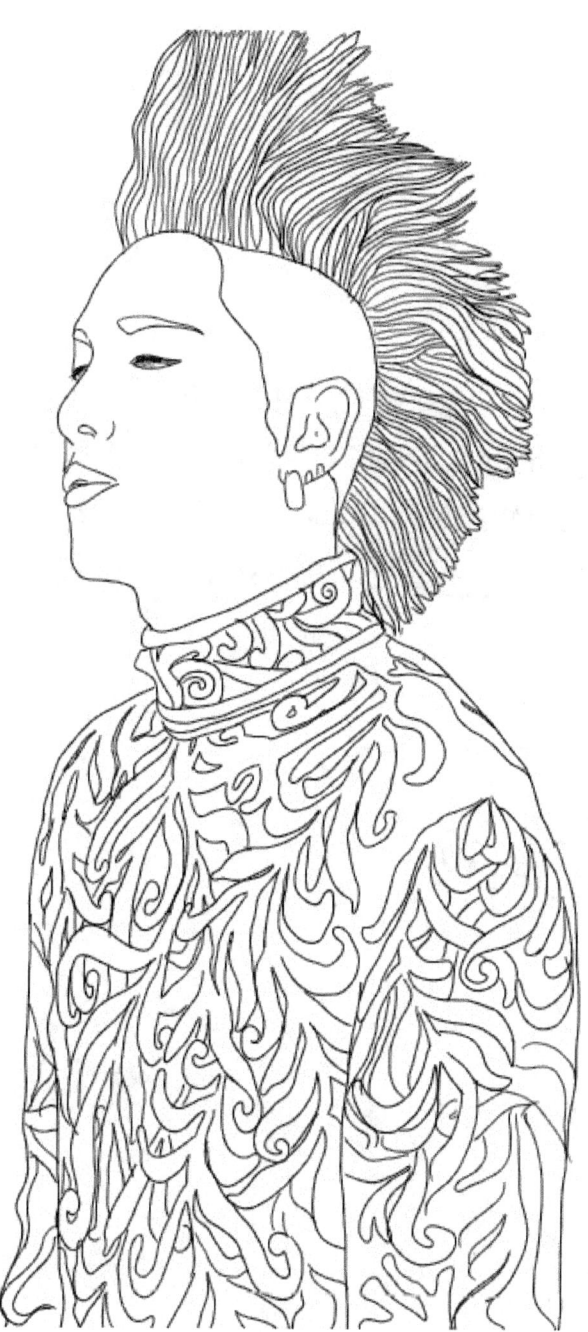

"I REALY LIKE MY EYES, NOSE, LIPS.
I ESPECIALLY LIKE MY NOSE. I REALLY
LIKE MY LIPS TOO. I THINK MY LIPS
ARE _____." —TAEYANG

A. FOXY
B. SEXY
C. PETTY

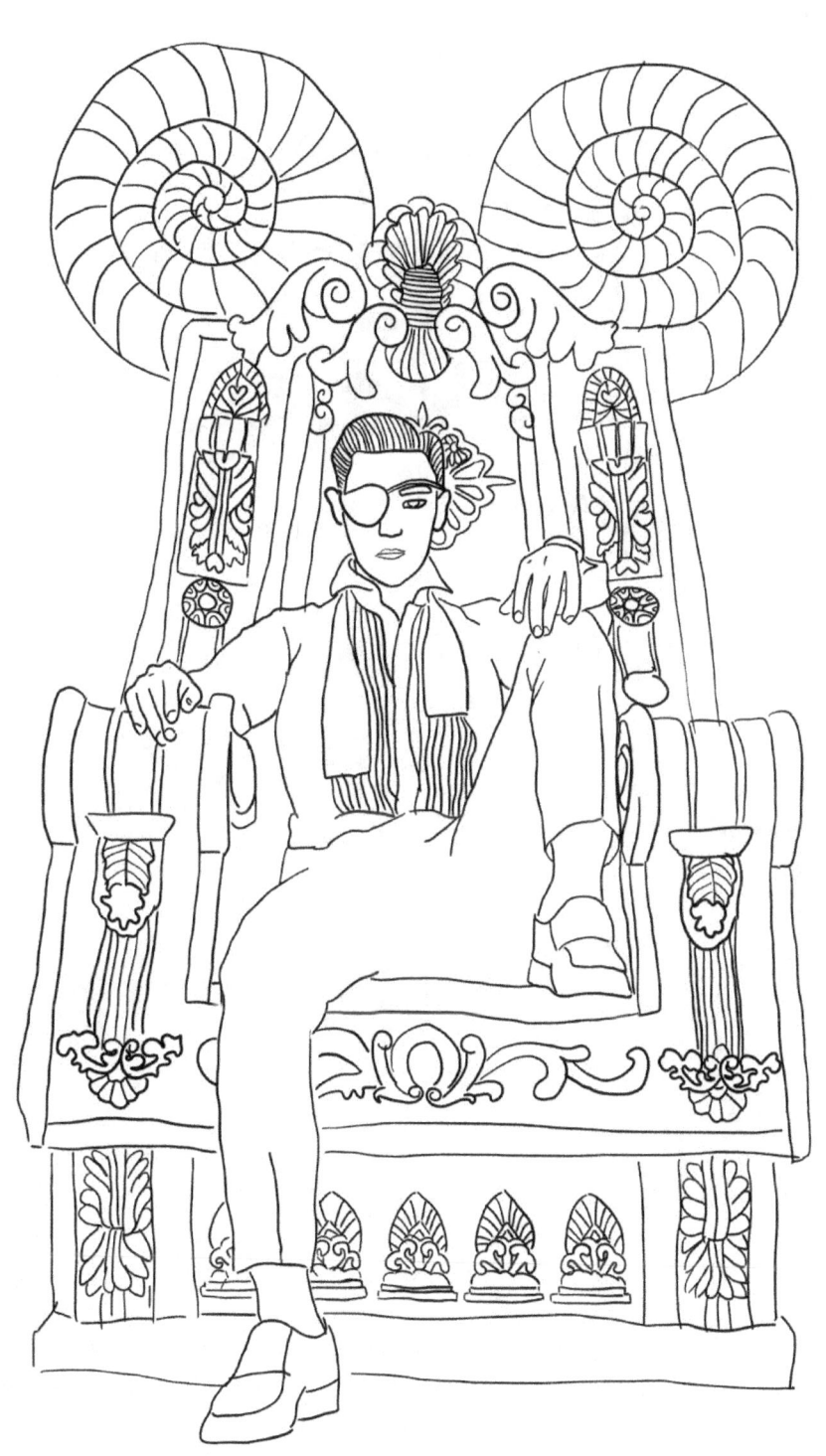

"BIGBANG IS JUST LIKE A _____ .
SO WE AIM THE SAME THING, NO
MATTER WHERE WE AT. " —T. O P

A. FAMILY
B. FREE WILLY
C. CAVITY

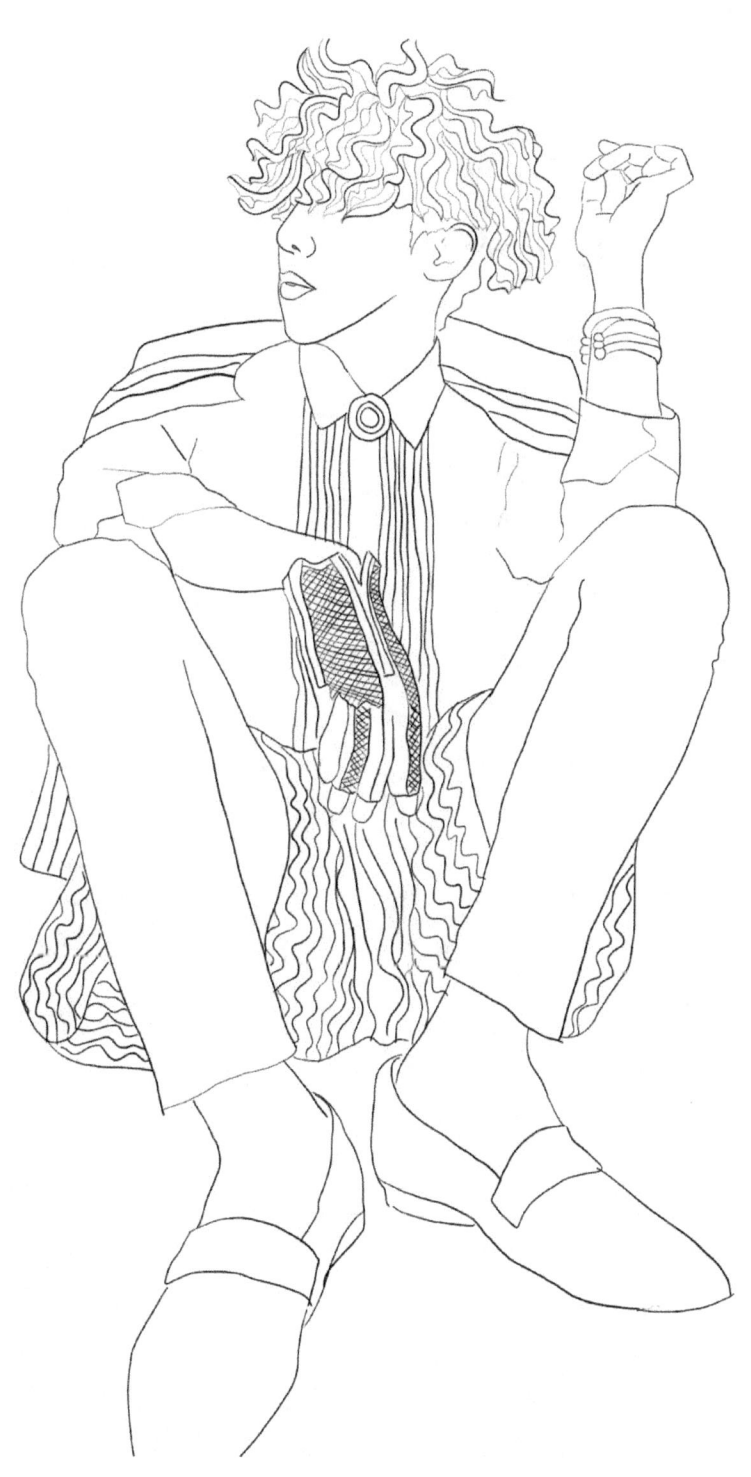

" I THINK A BEAUTIFUL PERSON
IS ONE WITH BEAUTIFUL _____ "
—GDRAGON

A. NIGHT
B. SIGHT
C. HEART

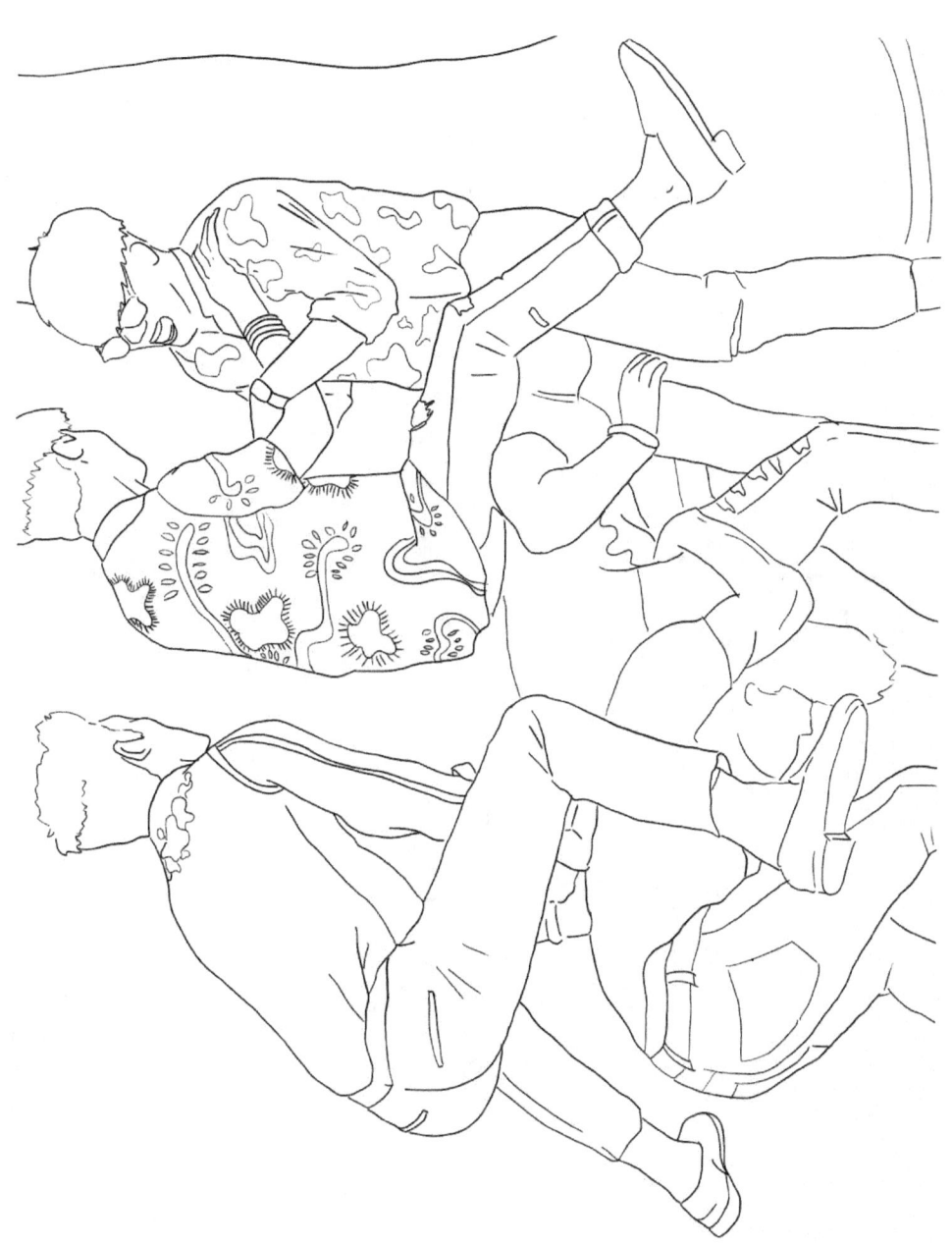

ANSWERS:

1. B
2. C
3. A
4. A
5. C

6. A
7. C
8. B
9. A
10. C

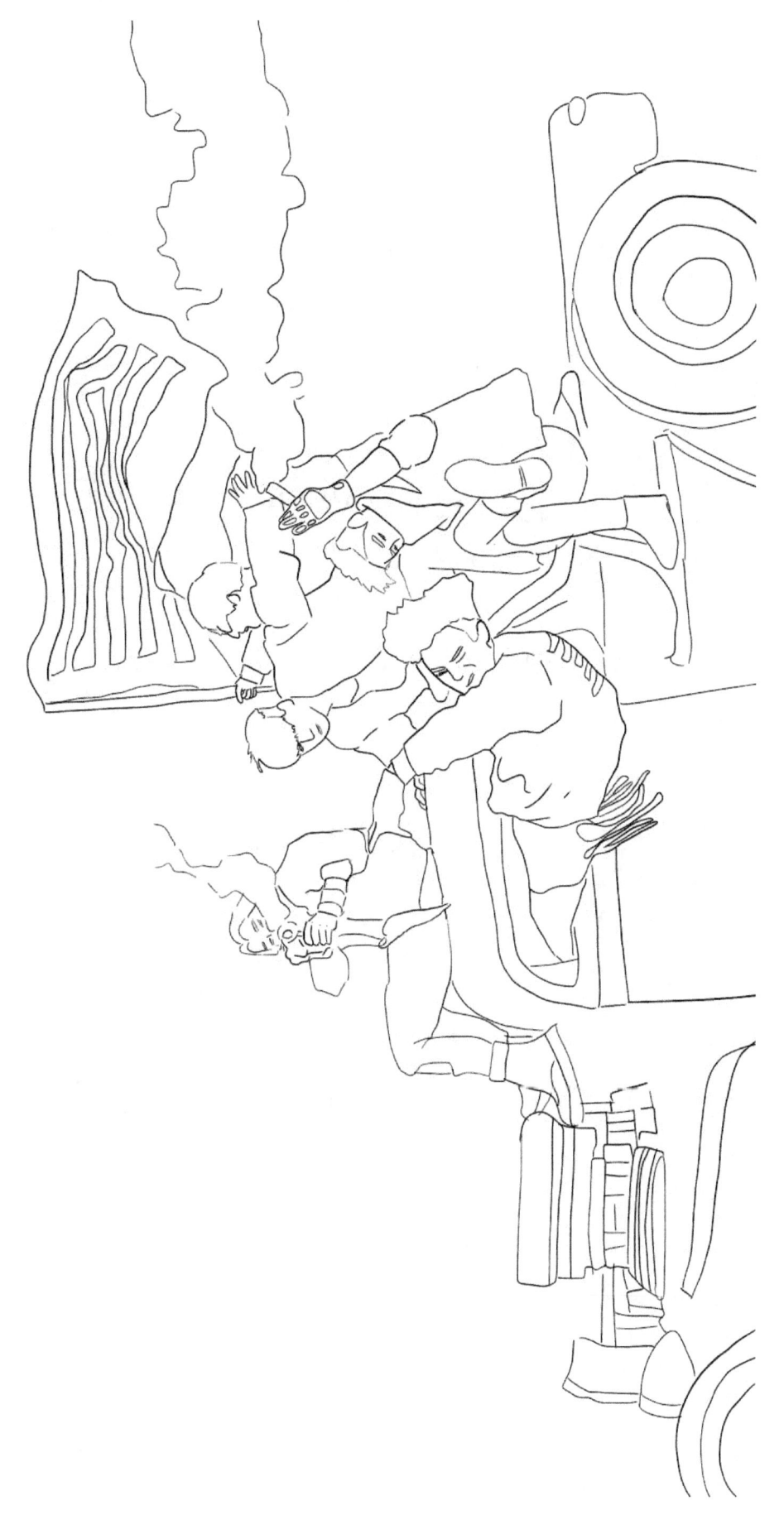

VIP BE LIKE :

    "ONLY DEEP MEANINGFUL LYRICS
    GET TO ME "

BIGBANG BE LIKE :

  "BOOM SHAKALAKA "

  "BANG BANG BANG "

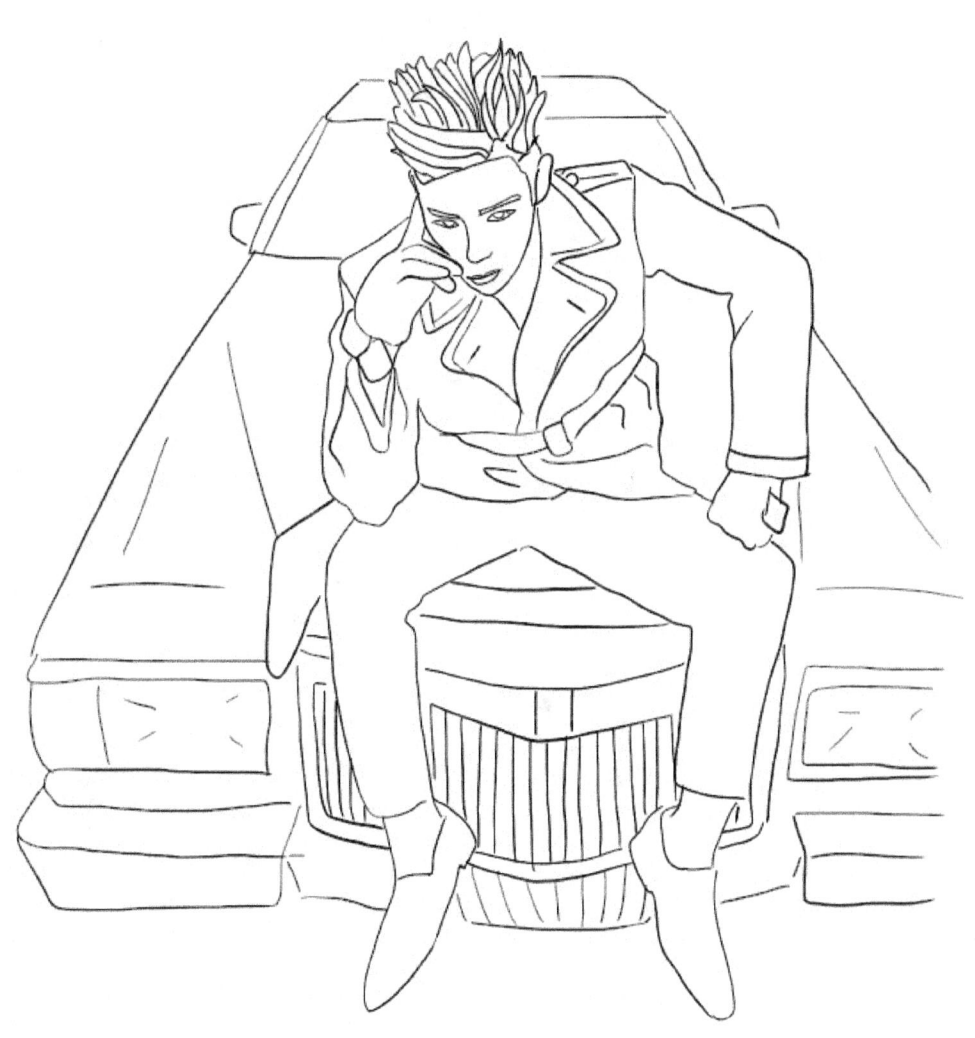

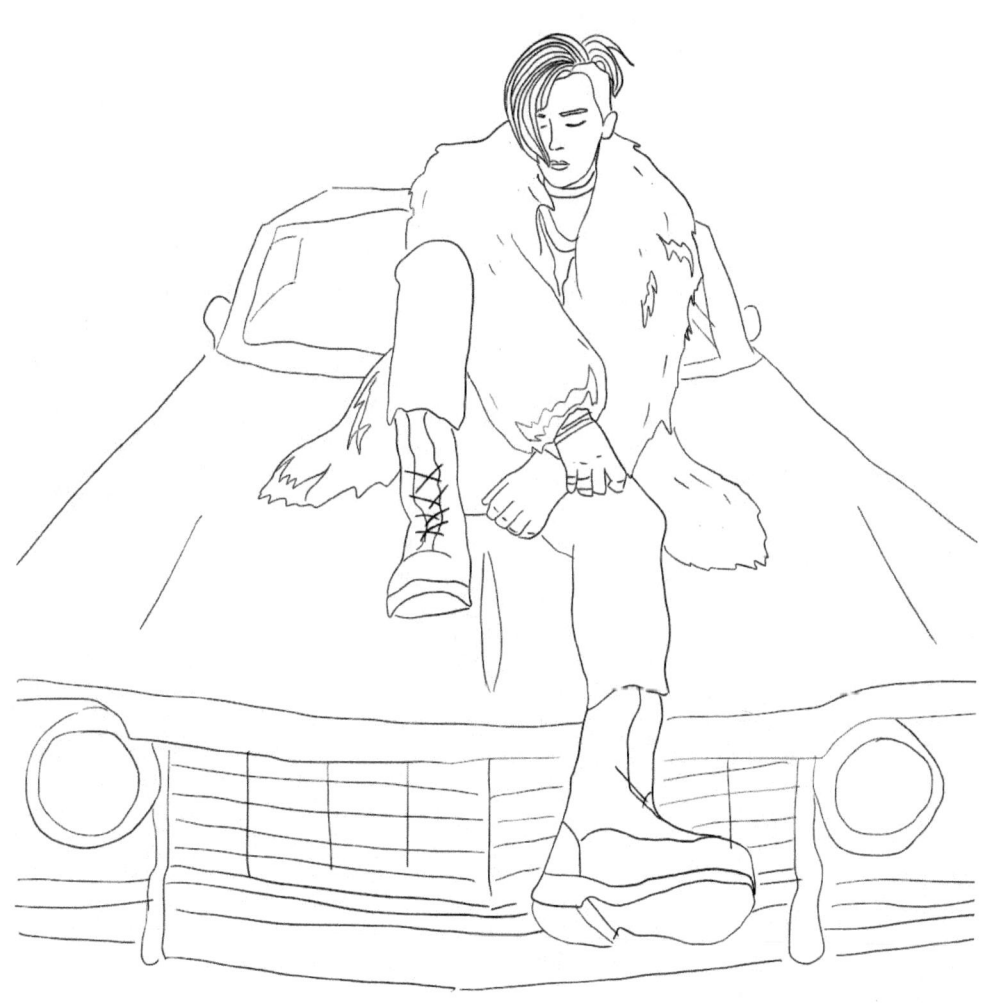

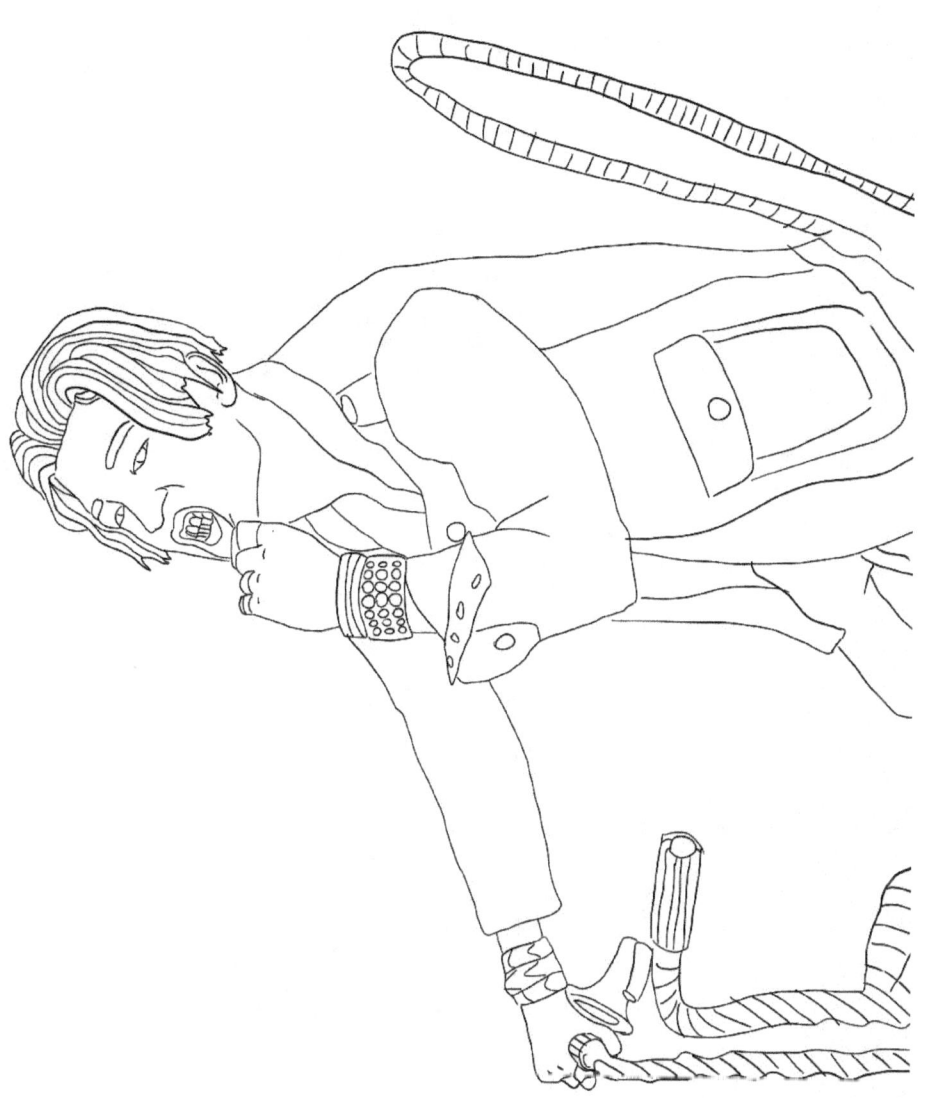

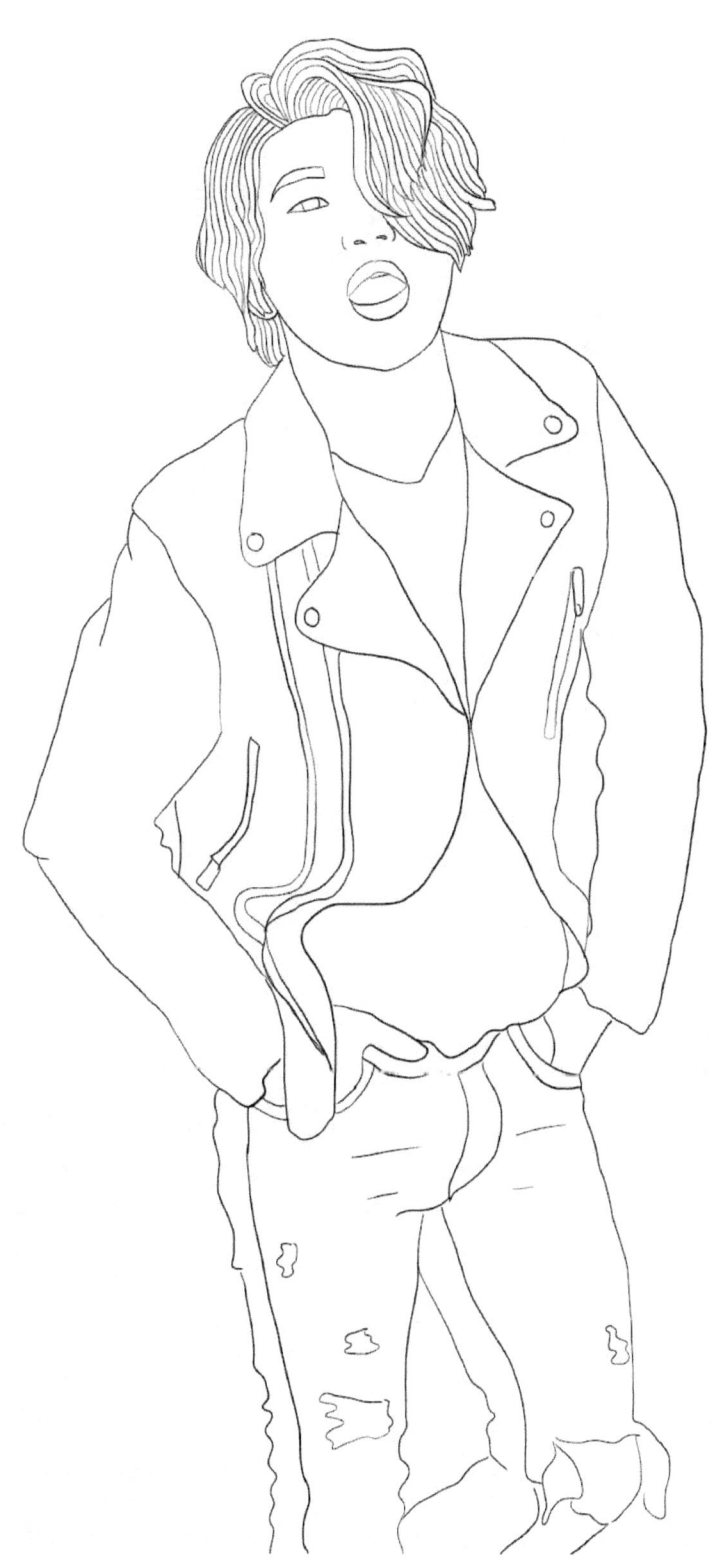

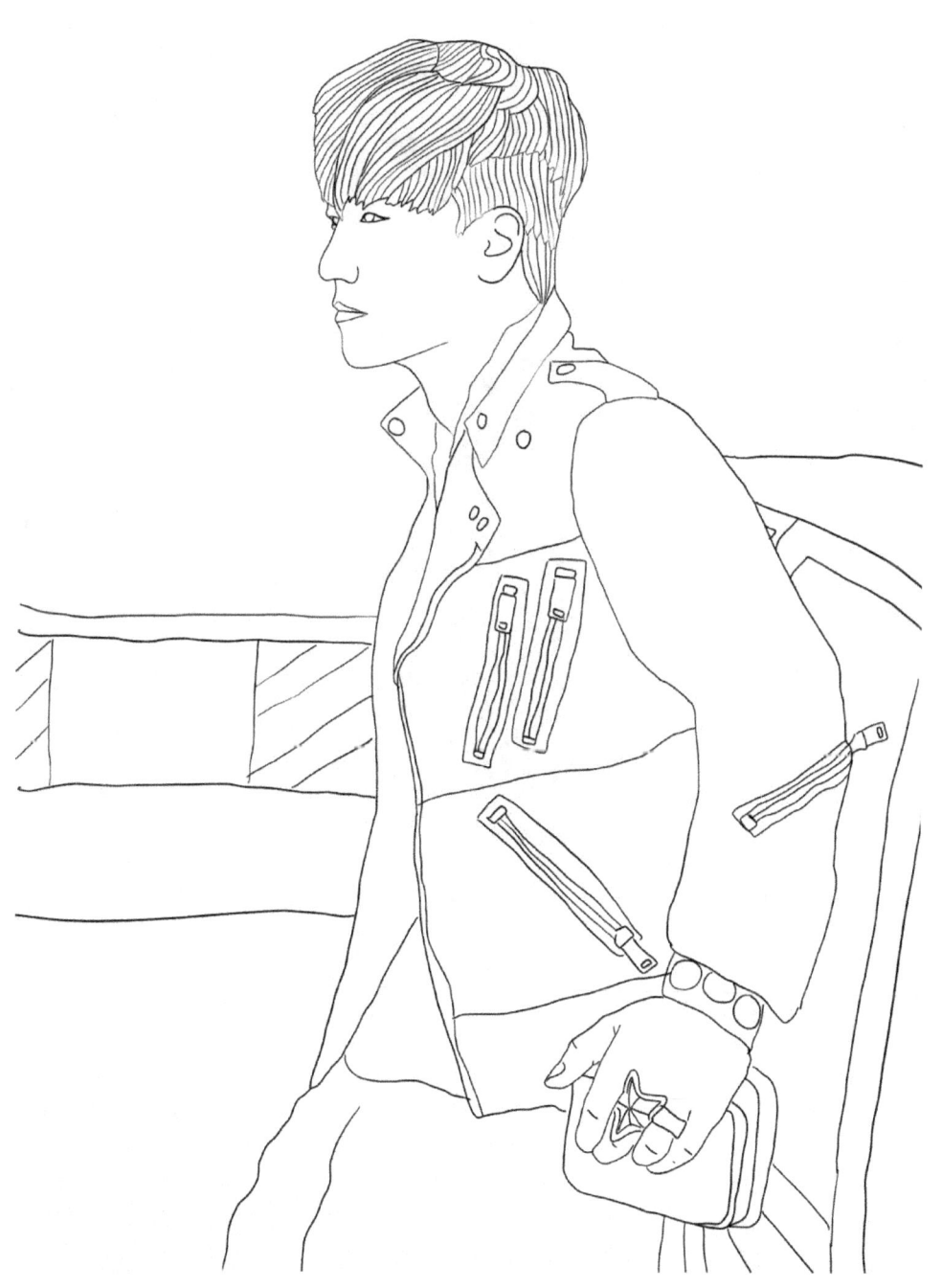

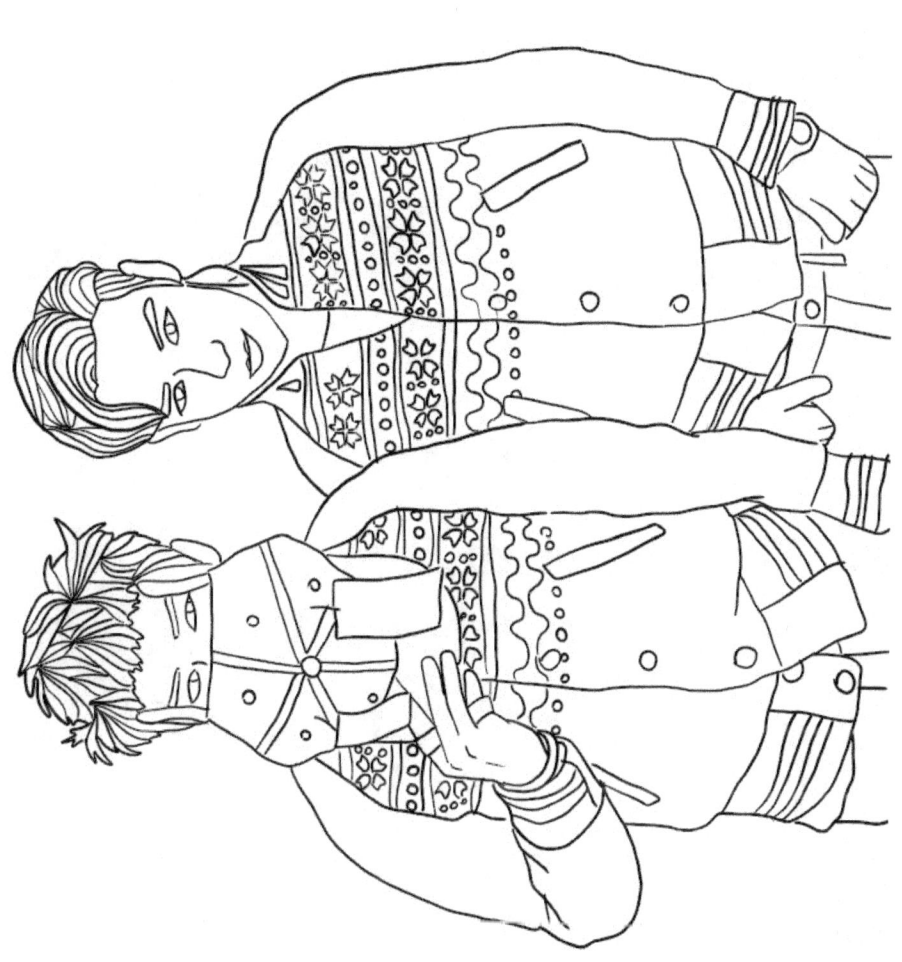

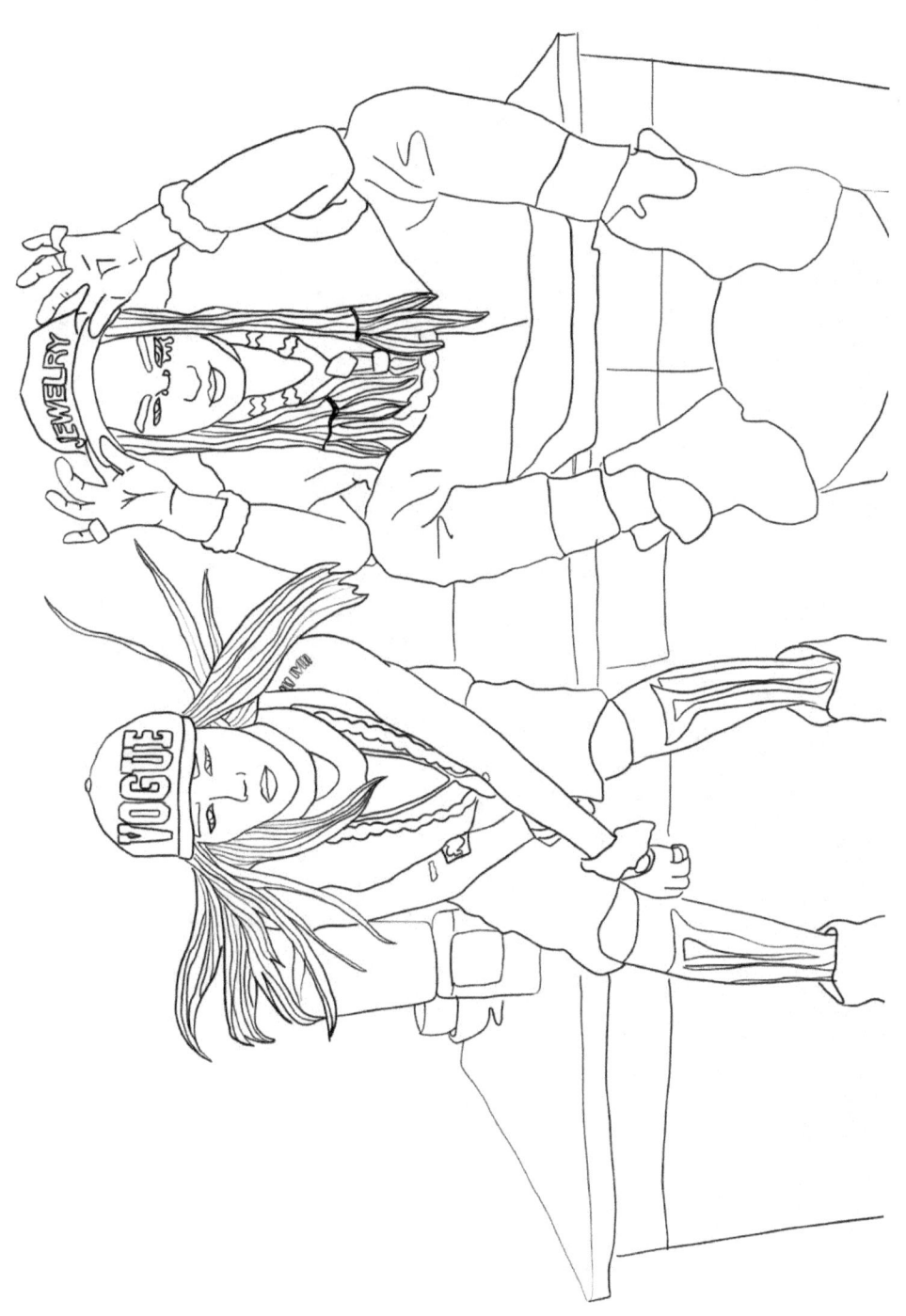

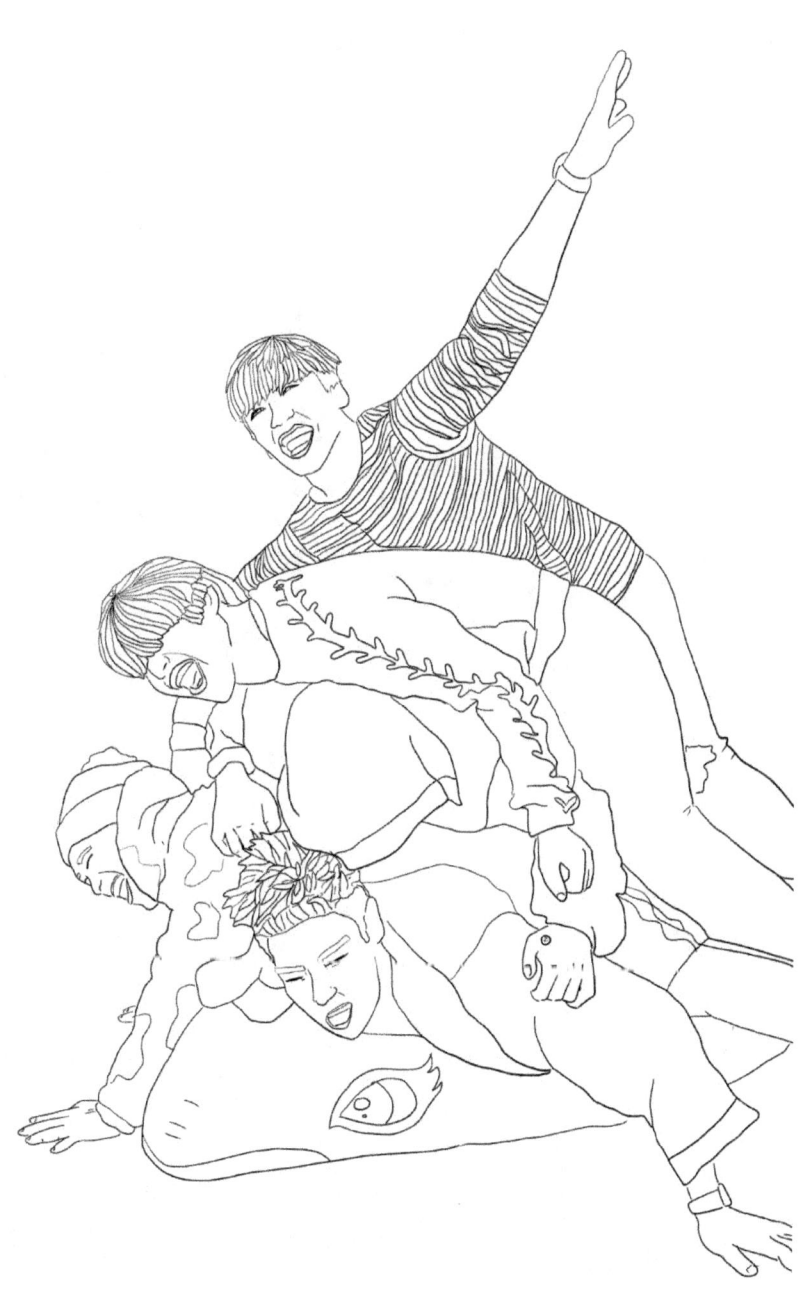

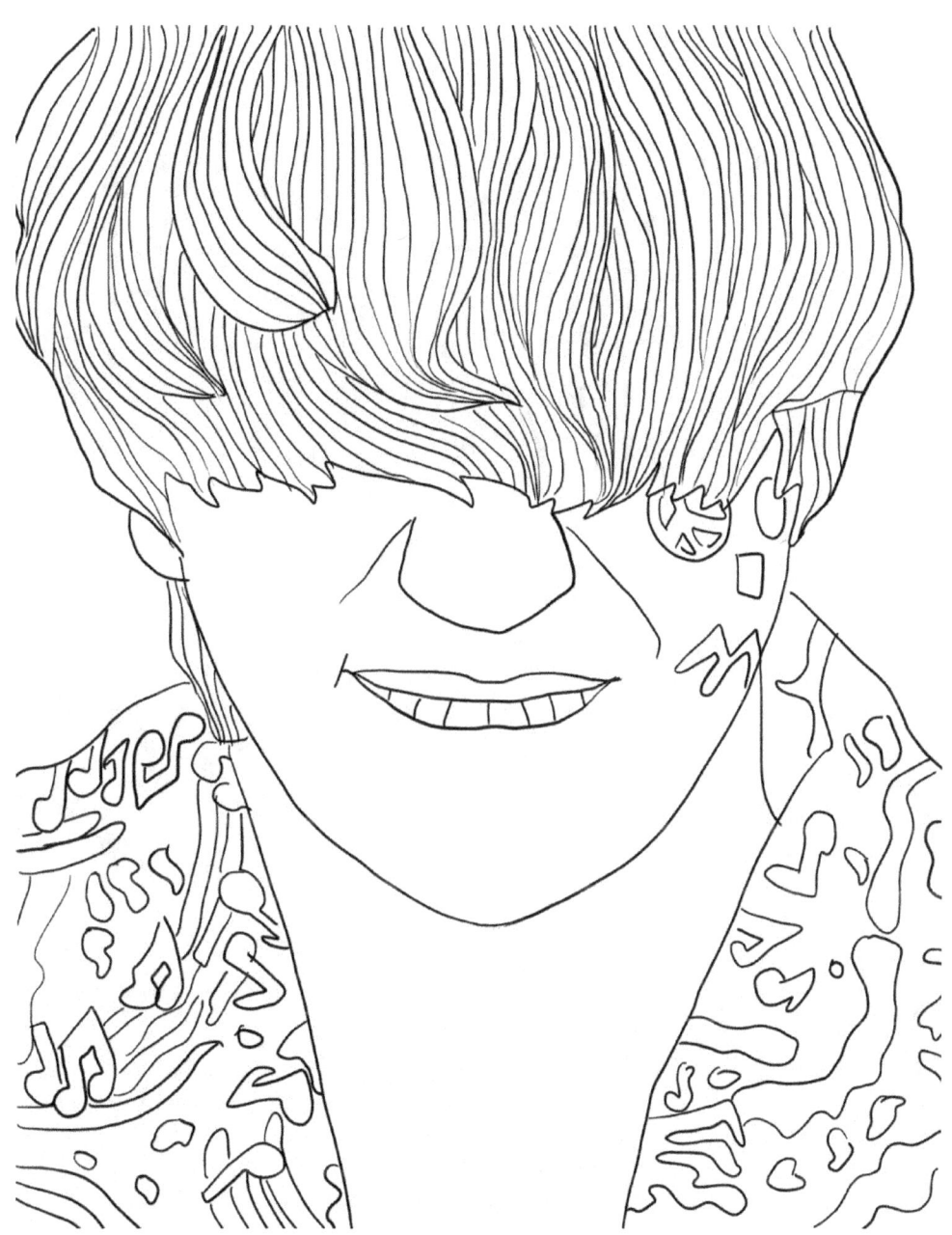

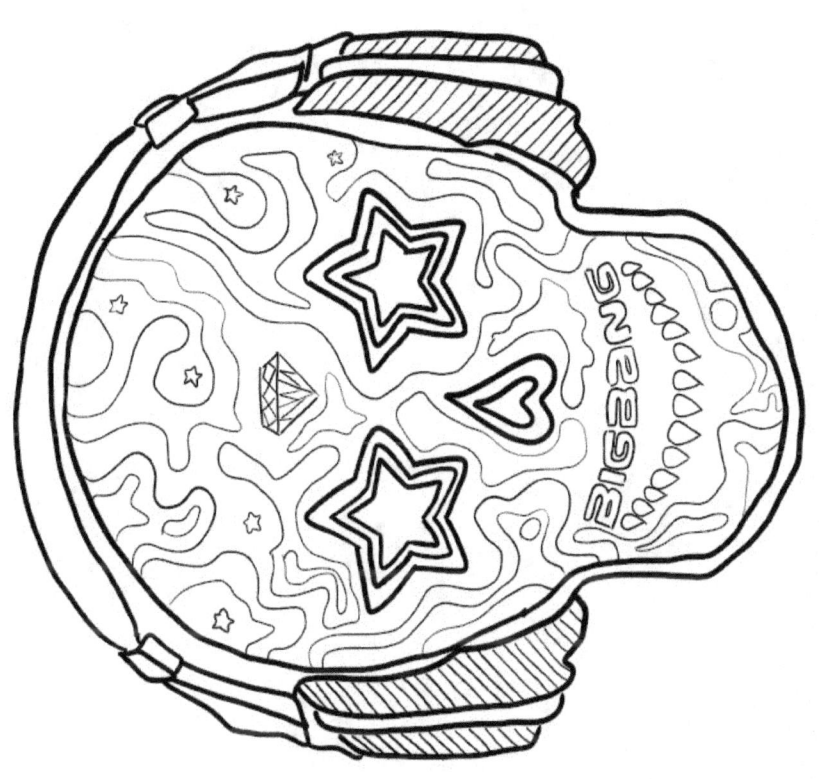

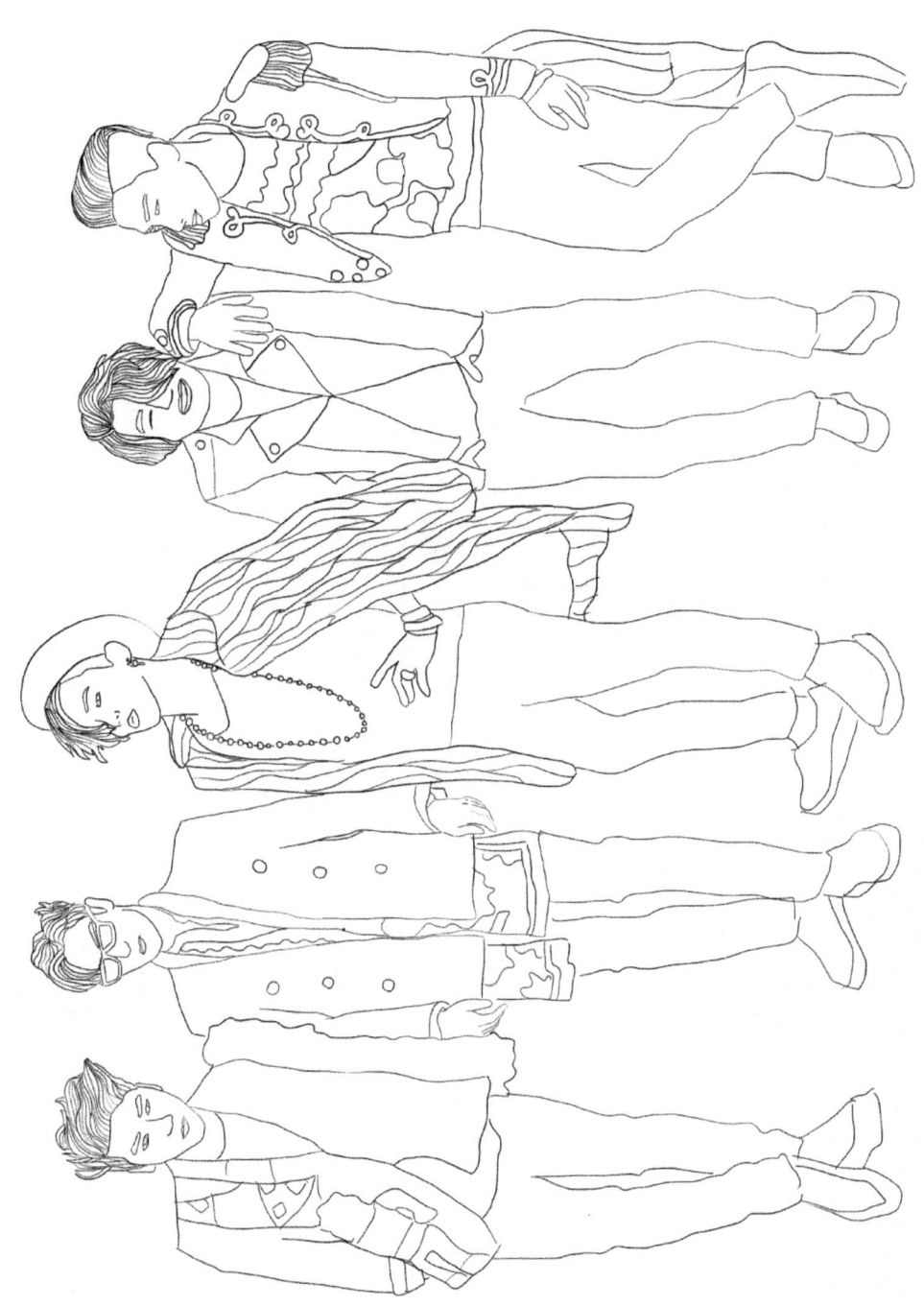

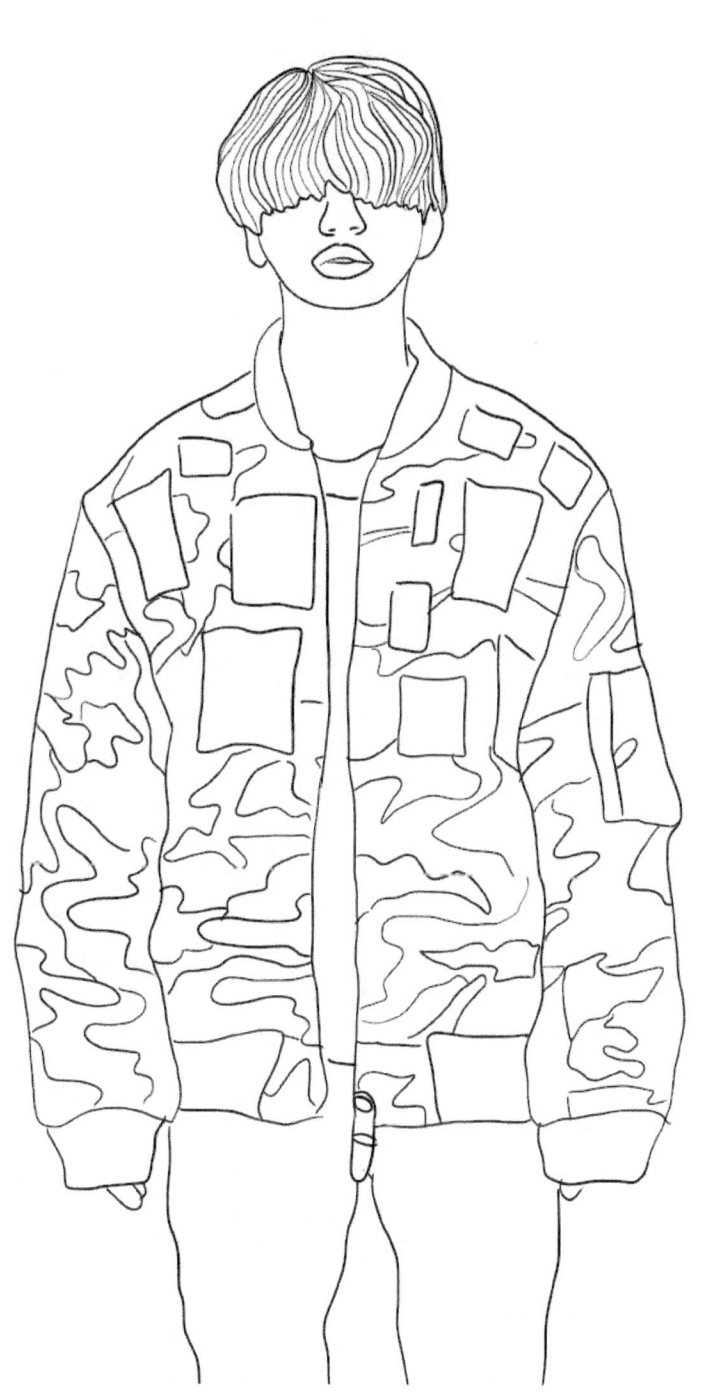

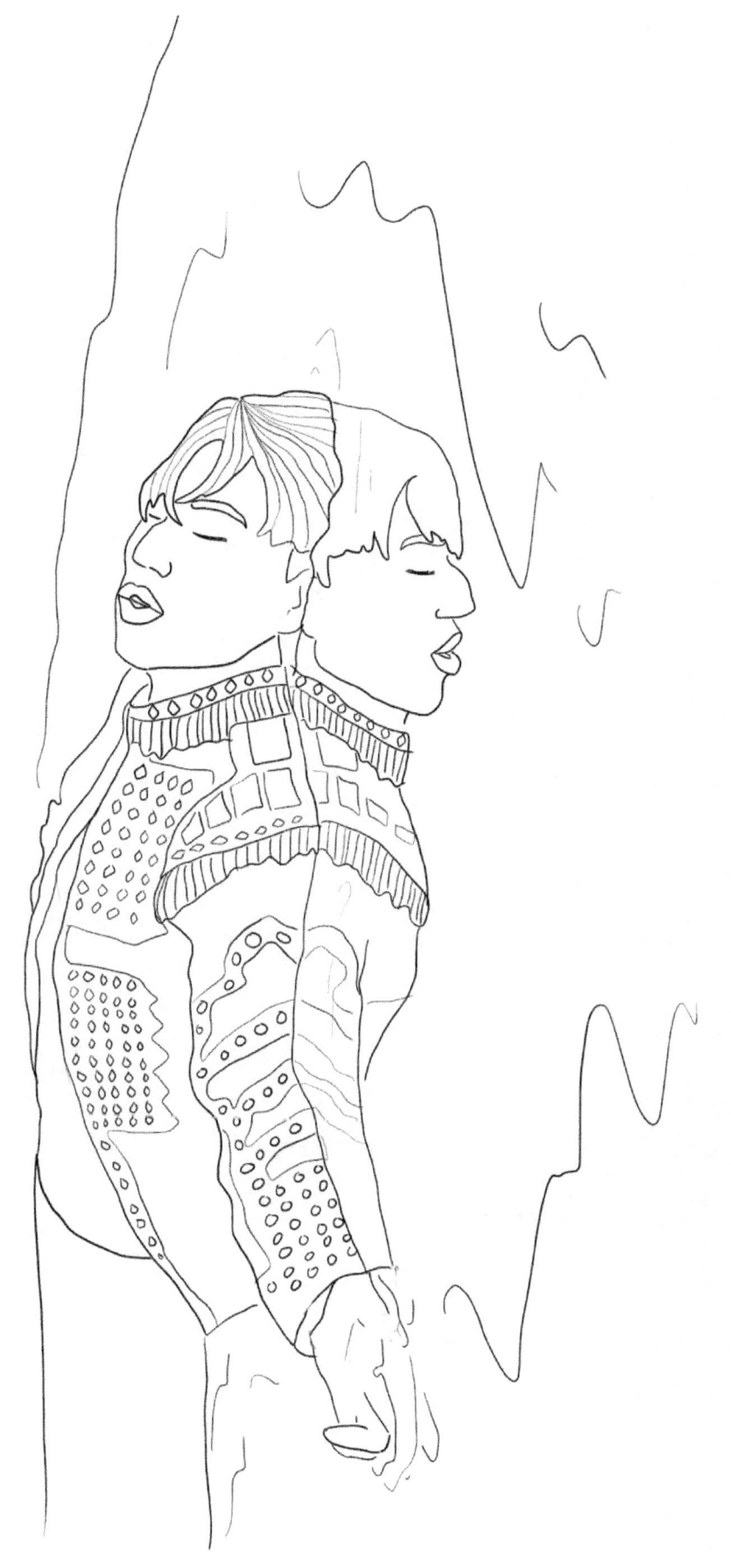

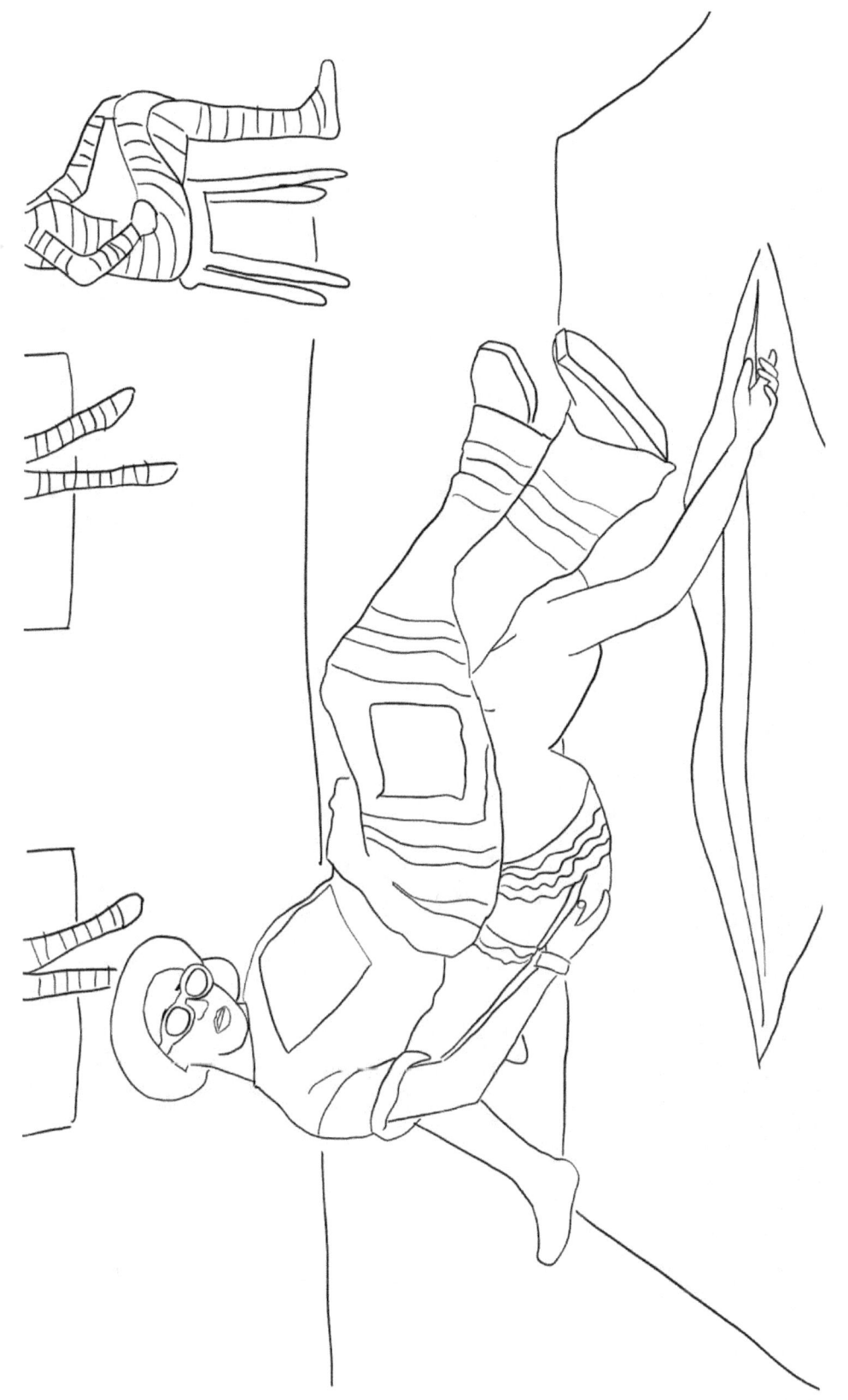

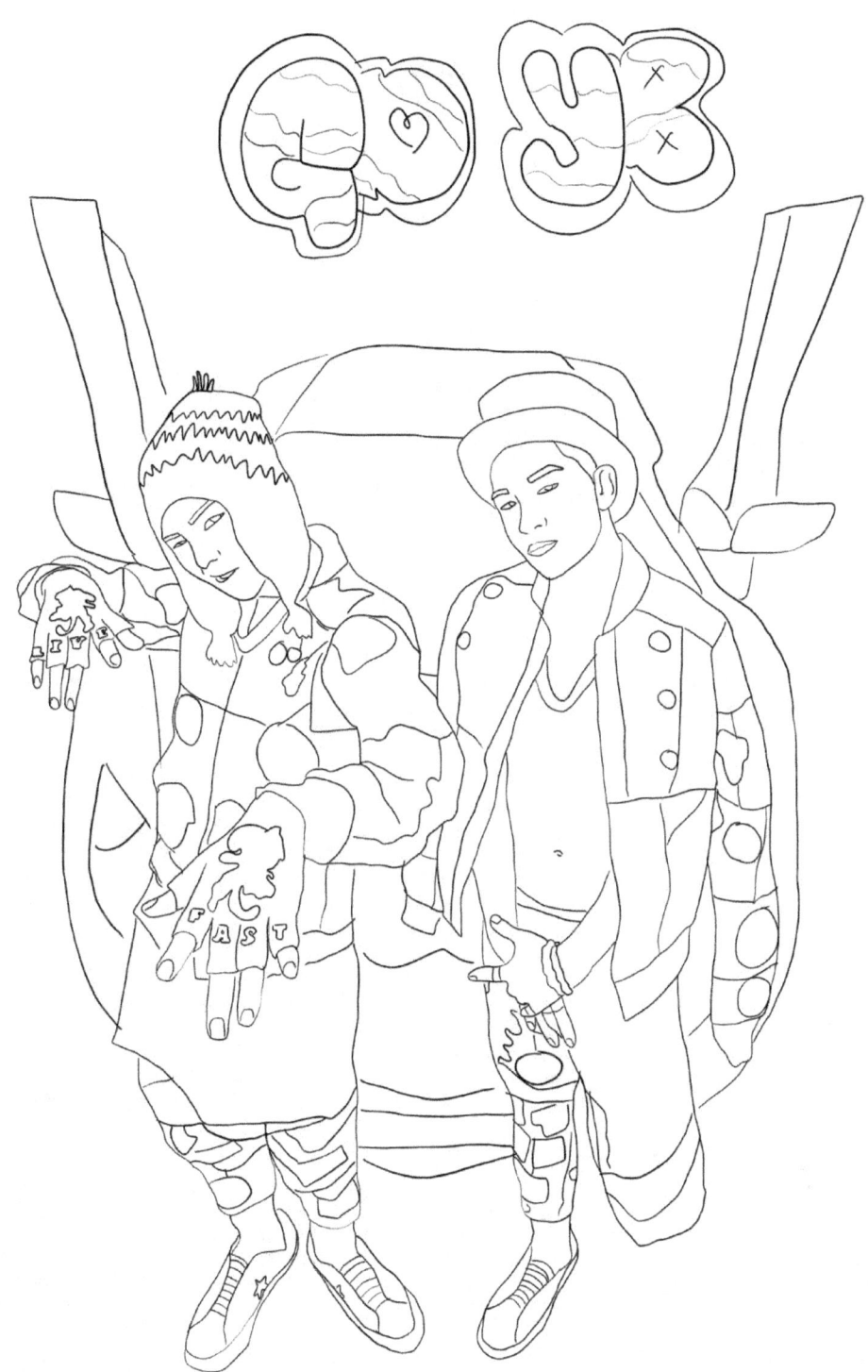

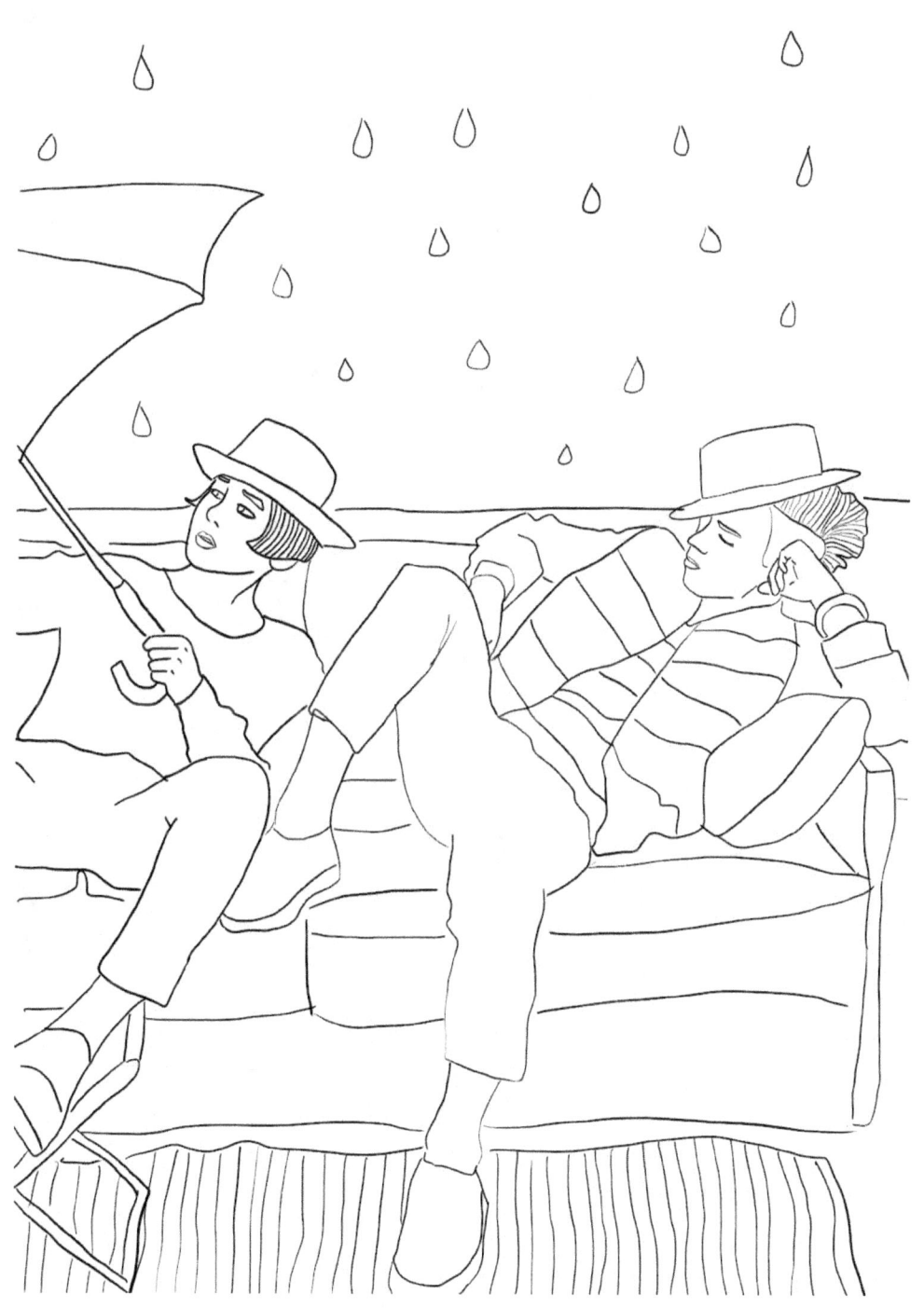

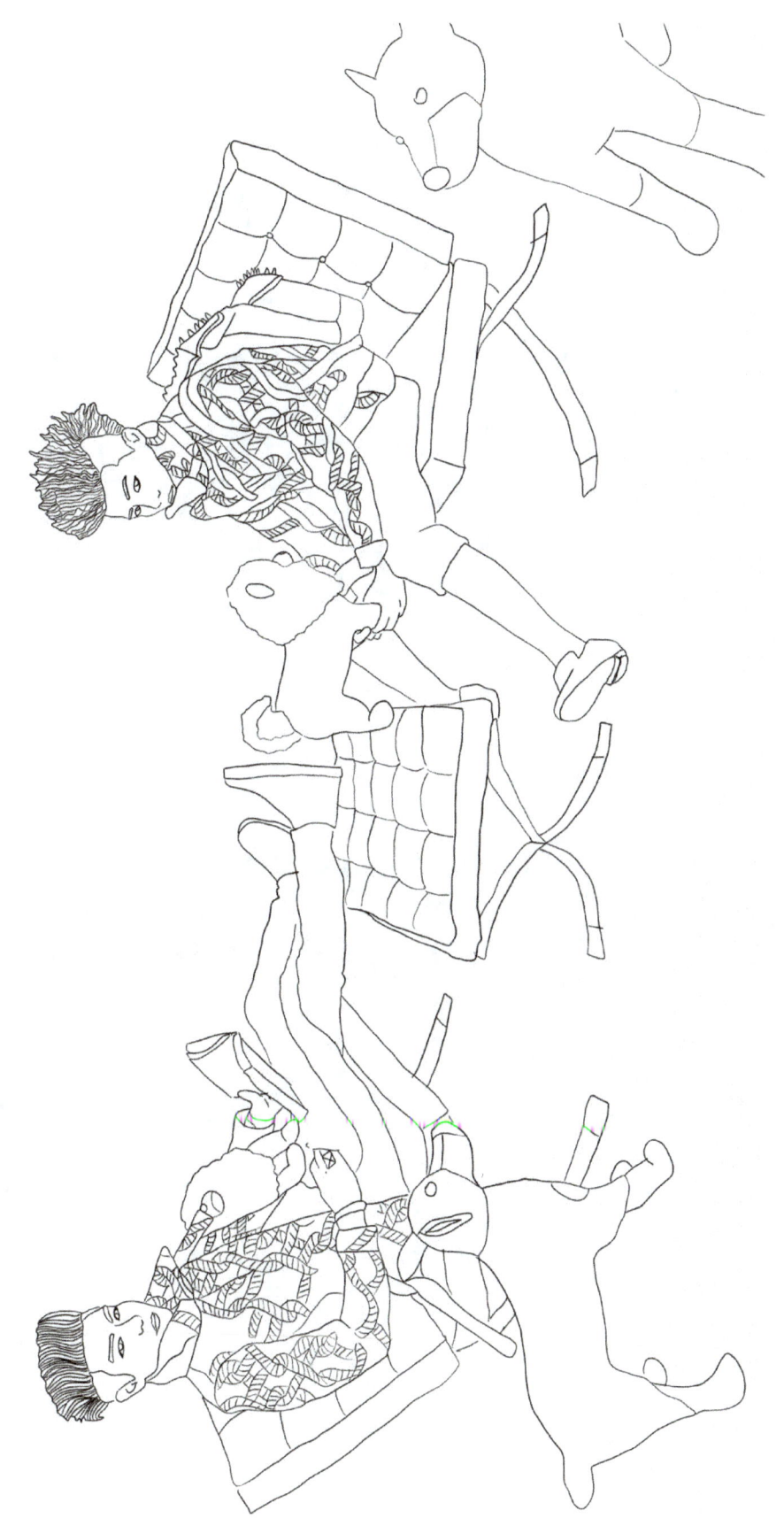

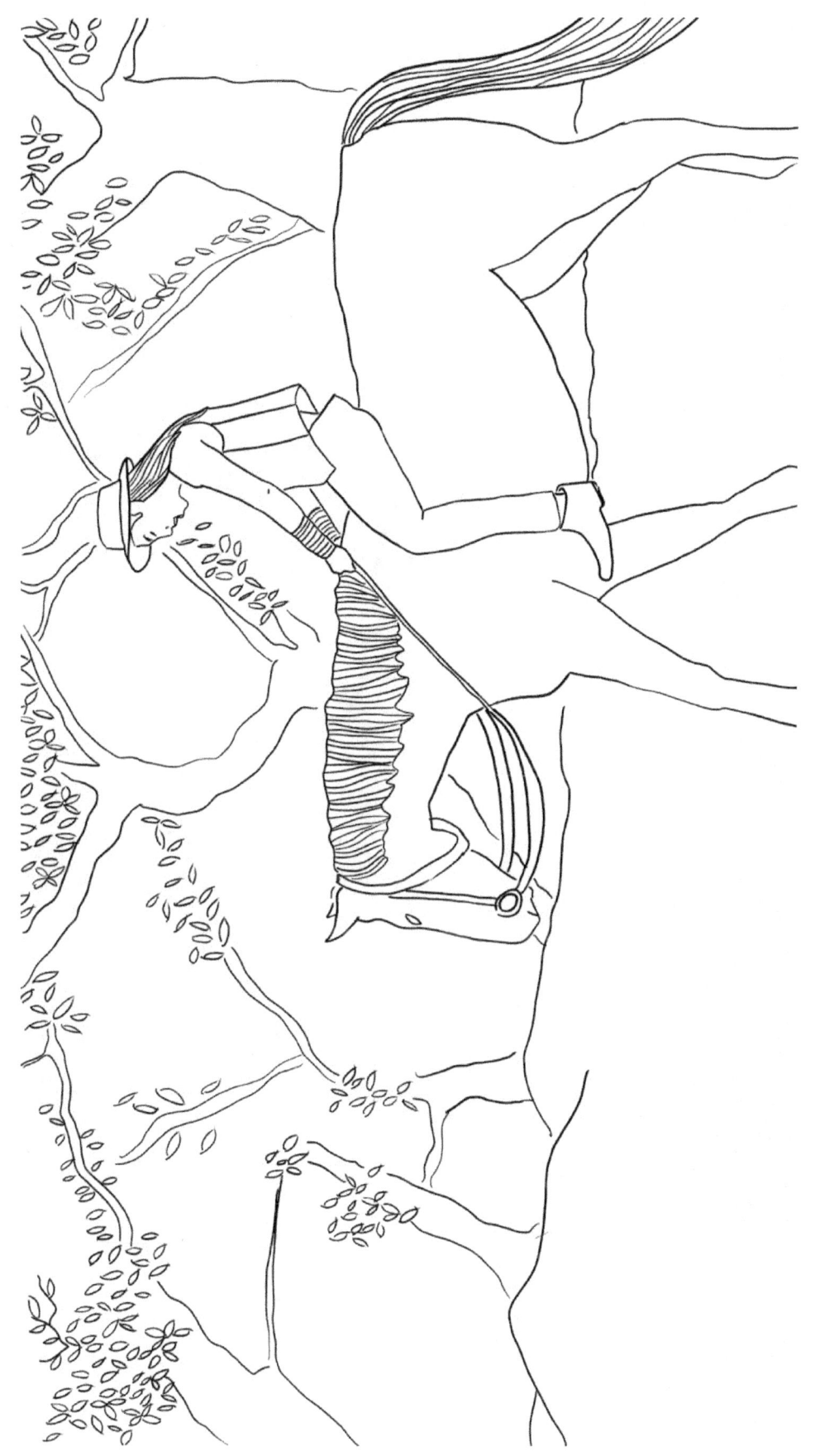

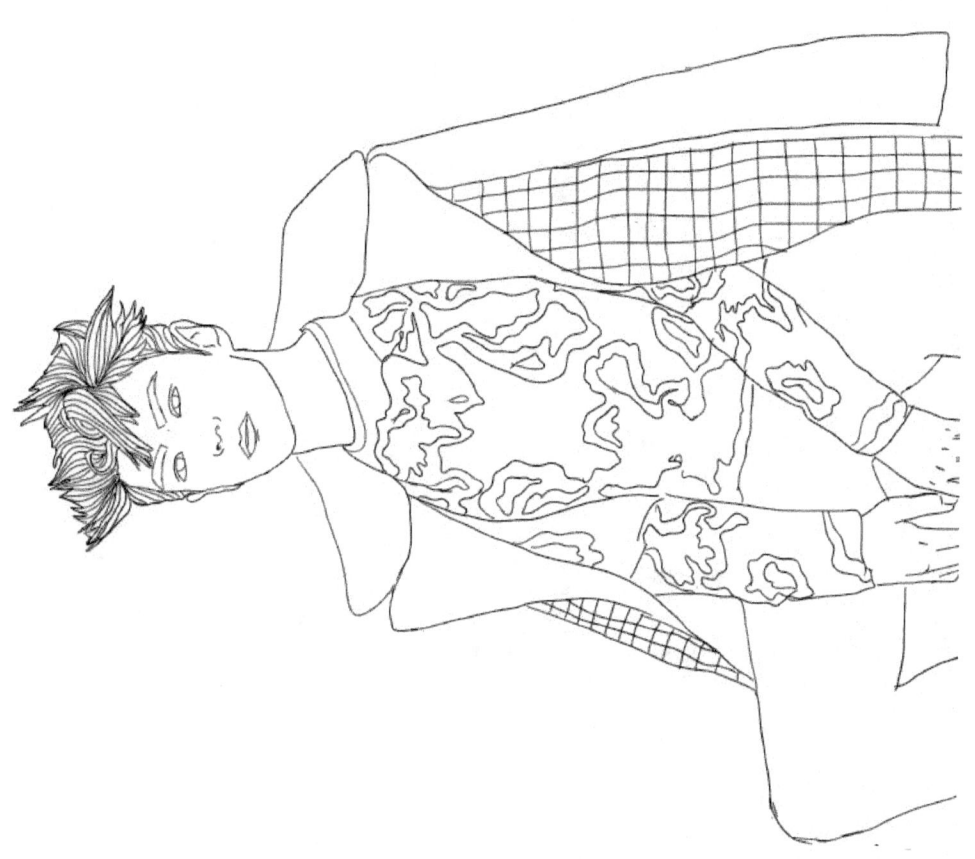

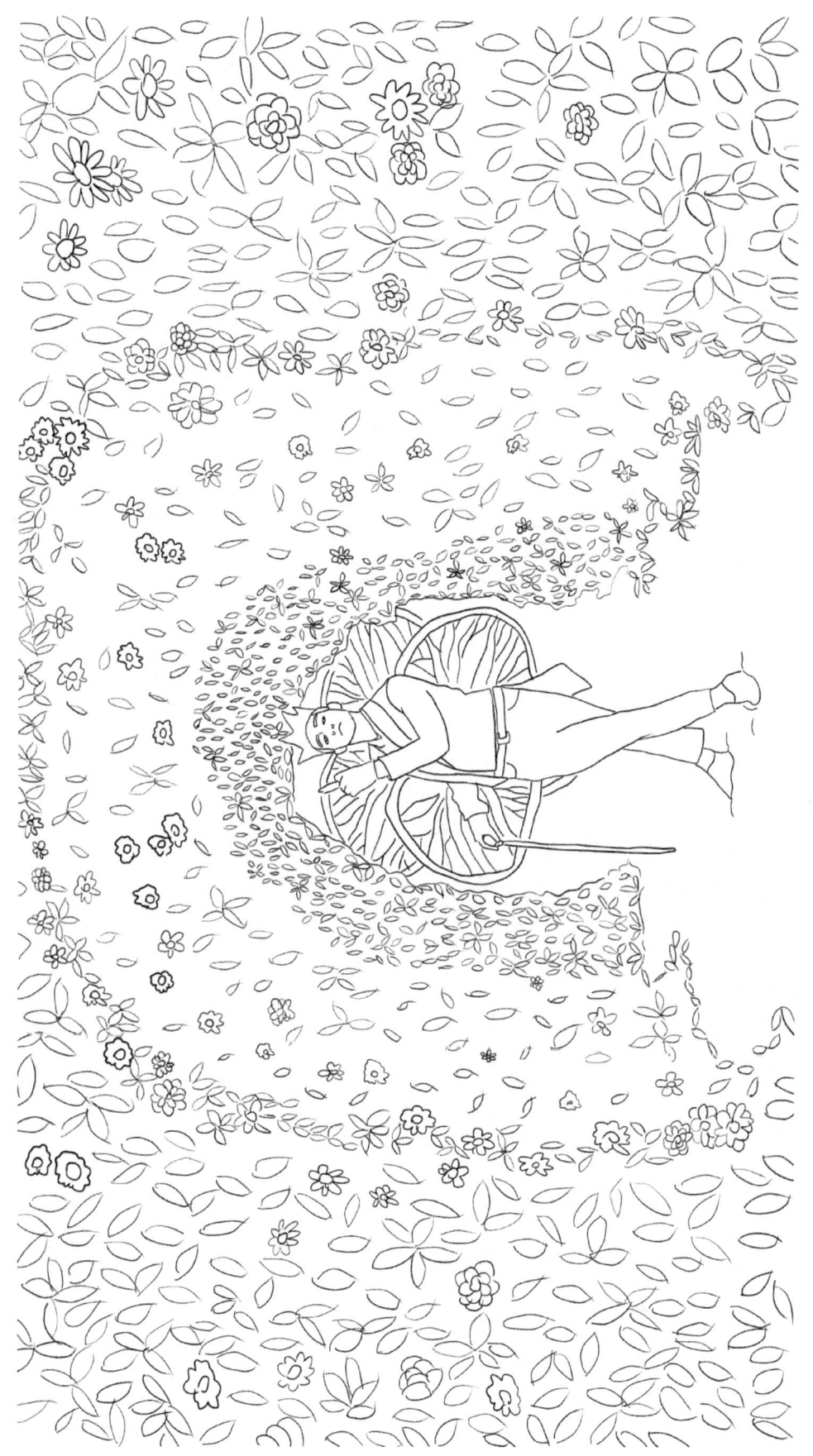

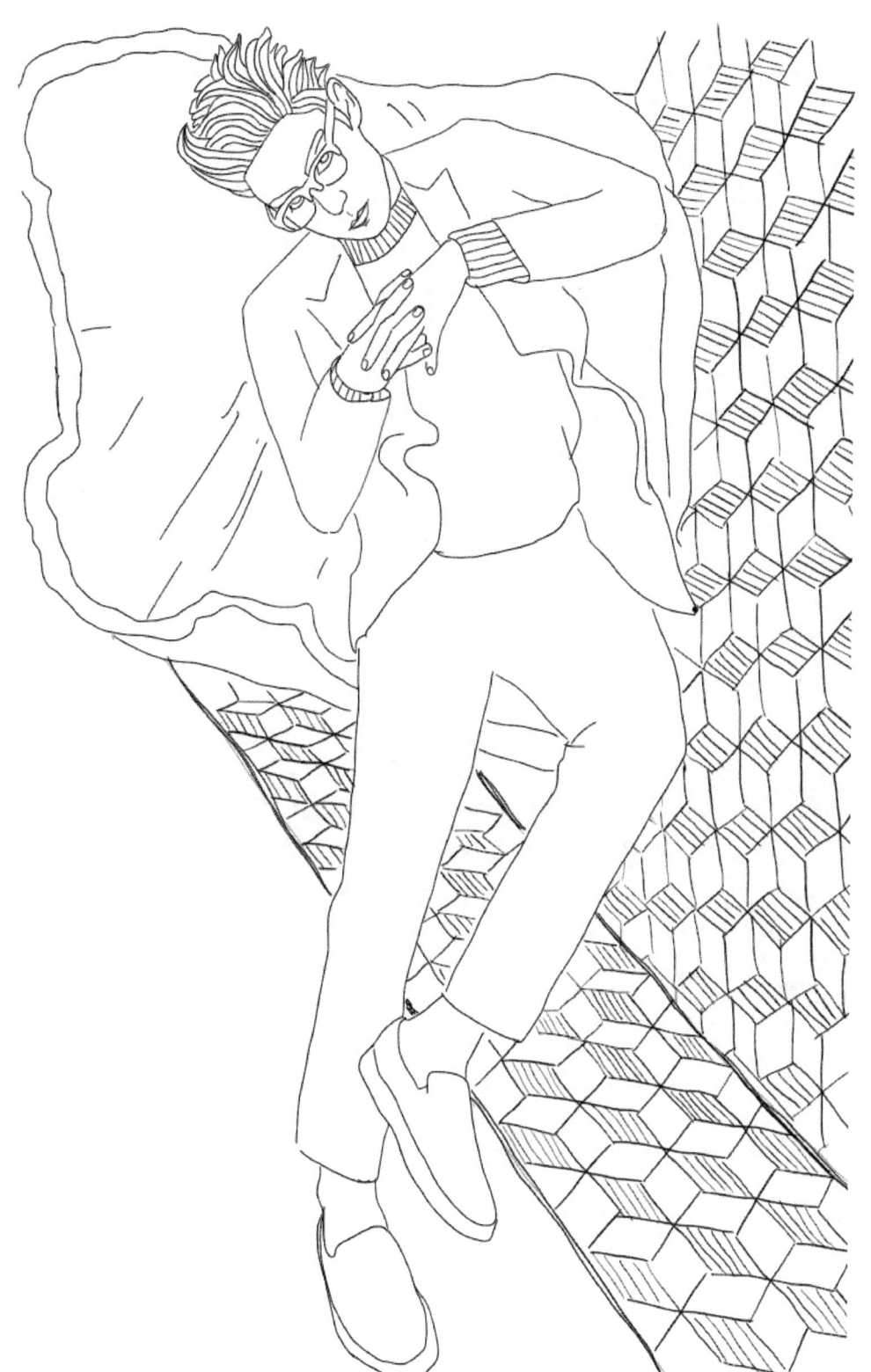

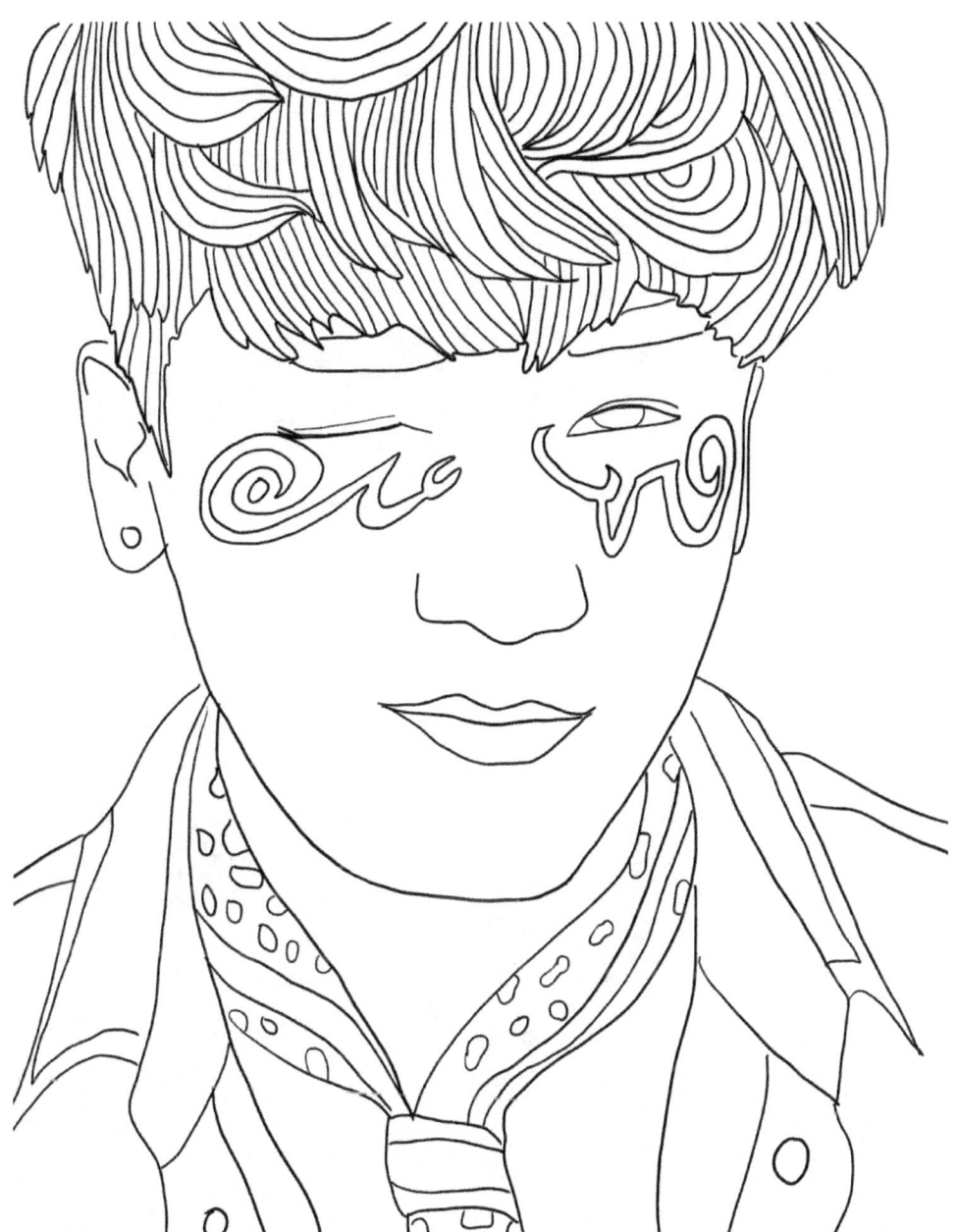

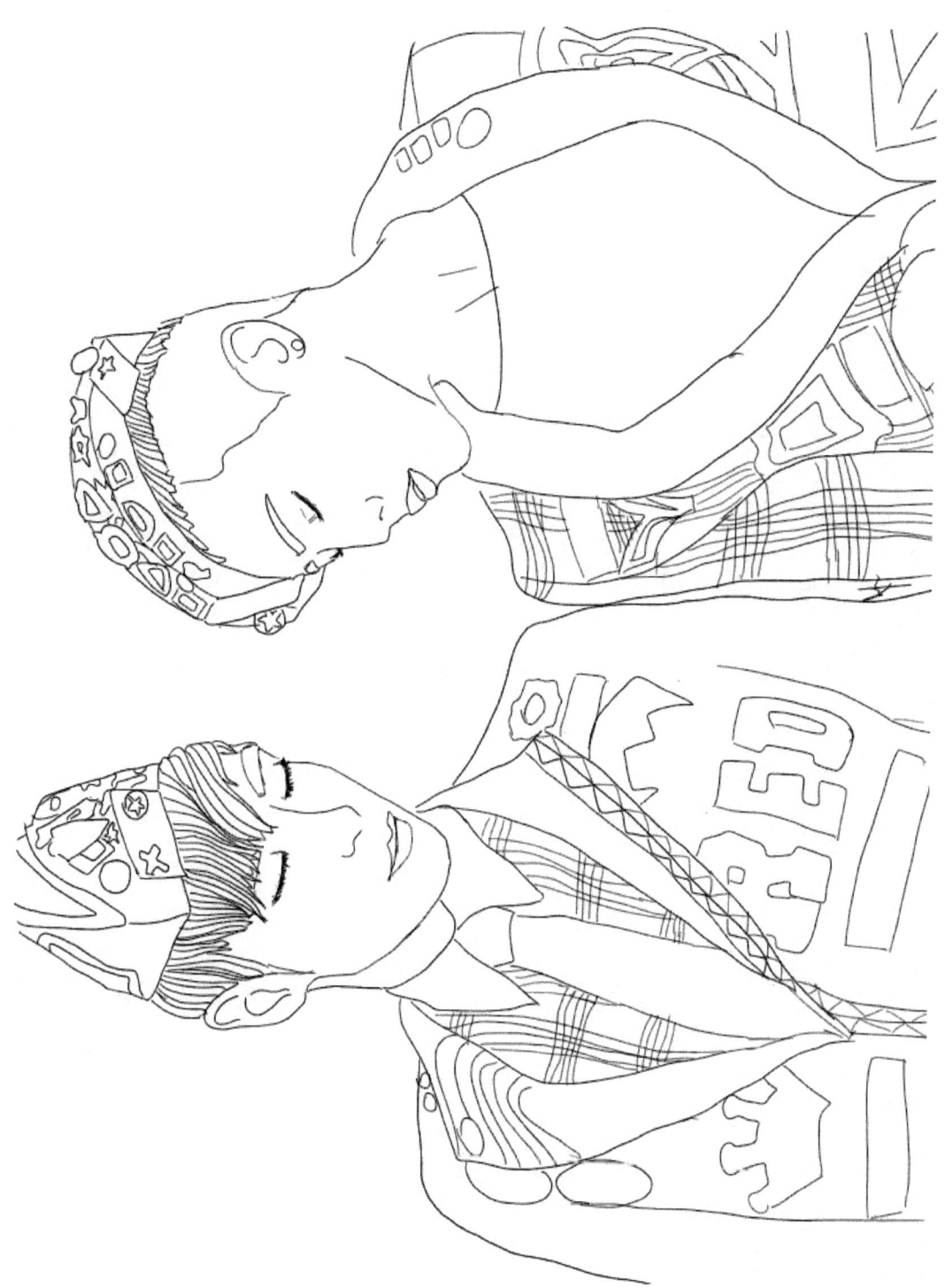

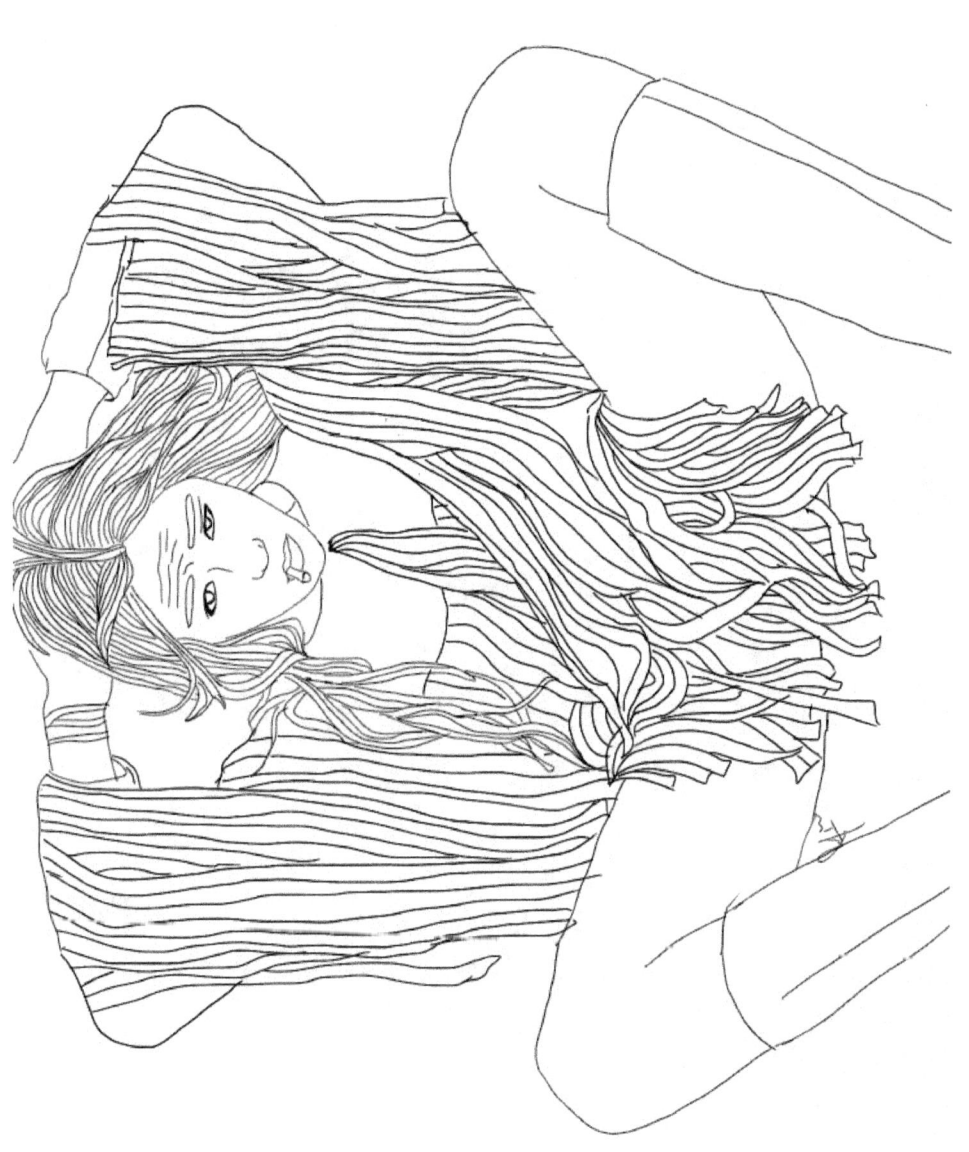

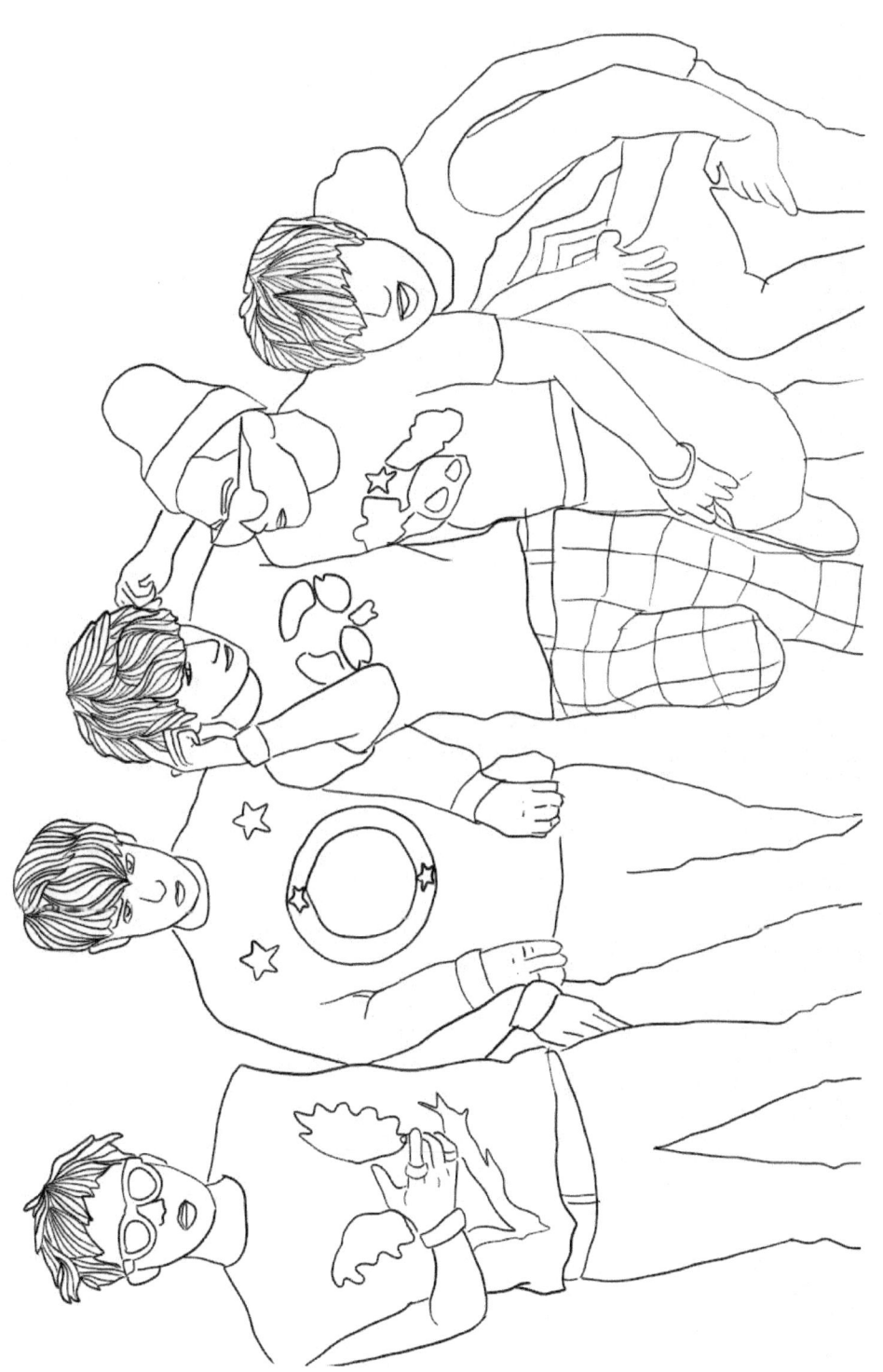

www.ingramcontent.com/pod-product-compliance
Lightning Source LLC
Chambersburg PA
CBHW081735170526
45167CB00009B/3829